IRISH MAIL

The Story of the 'Irish Mail'

The Royal Mail (London Train) to Ireland via Holyhead

William Davies

'The oldest named train in the world'

First published in 2016

© Author: William Davies
© Gwasg Carreg Gwalch

ISBN: 978-1-84524-254-1

Cover design: Eleri Owen
Top cover photograph: 'Irish Mail' by night, circa 1920
Bottom cover photograph:
150th Centenary 'Irish Mail' Virgin Train 43101;
image created by Mr Trevor Selby
from a photograph by Mr Mark Lloyd Davies.

Published by Gwasg Carreg Gwalch,
12 Iard yr Orsaf, Llanrwst, Wales LL26 0EH
tel: 01492 642031
email: books@carreg-gwalch.com
website: www.carreg-gwalch.com

I wish to dedicate this book to my wife My Dear Wife Ann for her love, support, patience and accord she has shown throughout the whole project.

Having now reached the twilight years of age, the last six of research and writing of the book has brought with it both purpose and pleasure, and the opportunity of making friendly and mutual acquaintances with numerous people, for which I thank them for their assistance and support

William Davies

Contents

1	Origins of the Irish Mail	9
2	The Age of Steam and the Arrival of the Railways	27
3	Laying the Line Euston to Holyhead	33
4	Three Bridges	58
5	Transference of Mails from Coach to Train	73
6	Formation of the London and North Western Railway	76

    Sub section
    (i)   L.NW.R.
    (ii) The Trent Valley Line
    (iii) Standard Time

7	The First Irish Mail Train and the Mail up to 1860	80
8	The Mail Steamer Contract	89
9	L.N.W.R. Locomotives of the Irish Mail	96
10	1860–1920	107

    Sub Section
    (i)   The Abergele Disaster
    (ii) The Tamworth Accident
    (iii) Passenger Facilities
    (iv) The building of the Holyhead Breakwater and Harbour of refuge
    (v) Development of the Holyhead Port 1860–1880
    (vi) Acceleration in Train and Ship Schedules
    (vii) The Weedon Rail Crash

11	1921–1964	144

    Sub section
    (i)   Grouping of the Railways
    (ii) Motive Power
    (iii) The Transition years
    (iv) The Penmaenmawr Crash
    (v) The Irish Mail Train Robbery

12 1965–2009   173
    Sub section
    (i)   The Britannia Bridge Fire
    (ii) Shipping Services
    (iii) Privatisation of Holyhead Harbour
    (iv) Rail Services
    (v)   Privatisation of the Railways
    (vi) The End Of an Era
13 Bibliography   193
14 References   197

Chapter 1

Origins of the Irish Mail

For the first main routes of communication across Britain we must go back to Roman times. They were exceptional road builders, laying down long and straight metalled surfaced roads for swift passage between garrisons throughout the country. One Watling Street, which started at Dover (Dubris) and went through Canterbury (Duroverum), London (Londinium), St. Albans (Verulamium), High Cross (Venonis), Wall, Staffordshire (Letocetum), to Wroxeter (Viroconium) situated five miles to the south of Shrewsbury. The road was 230 miles (368km) in length and followed a line similar to what the A5

'Holyhead Fort'
Section of the wall of the Roman Fort built about the 4th Century.
Within the walls can be seen The Collegiate Church of St Cybi.
Earliest parts of which were built in the 13th Century.
Author Collection

trunk road takes today. There is a general consensus that Watling St. extended across the whole length of the A5 road, whereas from Wroxeter (Viroconium) where there was a road junction it divided into a southerly route which ended at Kenchester (Magnis) in Herefordshire there it joined with another Roman road called Stone St. which led to the garrison at Caerleon (Inca Silurium) in South Wales. The other was a northerly route which led to Chester (Diva Victrix). From Chester a road was constructed across North Wales to Caernarvon (Segontium) passing through St. Asaph (Varis) and the fort of Caerhun (Canovium) five miles south of Conway. Although in Holyhead the walls of a Roman Fort still exist there was no evidence of a connecting road across Anglesey. However in 2010 an archaeological dig unearthed findings that suggested possibly a Roman road is buried across Anglesey.

When the Roman Empire collapsed and its legions were withdrawn from Britain in 410A.D. the country was plunged into what was called the 'Dark Ages' and the arterial system of roads built by the Romans went into disrepair and decline. It was to be another six centuries when after the Norman Conquest of Britain that the roads were resurrected, although in a basic form to offer a means of contact between their system of castle building.

To look for the origins of sea commerce and communication from Wales and the Western seaboard of the British Isles we must venture back into the annals of Pre History as far back as the Neolithic period, to an area around Penmaenmawr on the North Wales coast, where one of the most important sites in the country prevailed for the production of high quality stone axes. From there axes were transported throughout the country as far as S.E. England and Cornwall. Following in time, about 4000B.C. copper (Chalcoprite) was discovered and mined from open cast mines at Parys Mountain on Anglesey and at Ormes Head Llandudno, and shipped as far as Continental Europe. Mining continued until about 600B.C. when the mines were abandoned, only to be brought back into production in Roman times, before again being abandoned until the 18th century when once more production was restored. As further time passed around 2500B.C. saw the arrival of the Bronze age with Cornwall being a major area in the mining of tin (Cassiterite). Bronze being an alloy of copper and 20% tin which resulted in a harder and more resilient metal for tool and weapon manufacture. Cornwall thereby became an important area for the exportation of tin to Europe, and in 1100B.C. to the Mediterranean by means of the Phoenicians (from Lebanon) who were renowned sea traders in the Middle East, who having ventured into the Atlantic waters established the port of Cadiz/Gadir in Spain thereby giving the opportunity of commerce with Cornwall.

Over the course of time from about 600B.C. and the Iron Age period the Celts began to migrate from Central and Western Europe and settle in seven important areas, Wales (Cymru), Scotland (Alba), Isle of Man (Mannin), Ireland (Eire), Cornwall (Kernon), Britanny (Breizh), Northern Spain and Portugal (Galicia). The Celtic people were highly skilled in iron work production, which resulted in an expansion of both overseas trade and communication. Also the Roman invasion and conquest of Britain in A.D. 43 brought with it further expansion of coastal settlements both in military and civilian terms. As in Holyhead, other forts were sighted on navigable rivers and estuaries and the first harbours of any importance were built in order to defend and maintain their occupation. Therefore importation and exportation of goods and supplies was essential. There is speculation that the Romans invaded Ireland, whereas in general they never occupied it. However there is evidence that the remains a Roman fort or maybe trading station was sited not far from Dublin and that Roman artifacts were also discovered. However it is likely that commercial and cultural links existed between the Romans and Ireland. An example of this is highlighted by bi-lingual inscriptions in Latin and Ogham (old Irish alphabet) on memorials both in S.W. Wales and S.E. Ireland.

The withdrawal of the Romans from Britain in 410A.D. saw the diminish to an extent in overseas trade. In general this in it self played a part in the renewal of maritime links in the early medieval period based around the Irish sea and the West coast of Britain, relating to which was the distinct Celtic Christian culture. This progressed into the Post medieval and Tudor period of a growing population and coastal activity. This growth therefore brought to the fore a requirement by which to quickly communicate and maintain state affairs across the country.

Consequently in the 16th Century, Henry VIII established a system by which he could dispatch and receive official messages to and from his representatives throughout the country as speedily as possible. In order to do this a series of stations called 'Post Houses' were built and situated along the roads at specific distances where horses could be stabled, in order that it allowed the King's messengers carrying the Royal dispatches to change to fresh horses as quickly as possible.

When Queen Elizabeth I came to the throne it was necessary for a line of communication to be implemented between London and the Queen's Lord Lieutenant in Ireland. With this the Queen's messengers or 'Post Boys' as they were then called proceeded to carry their 'Mail' to Liverpool in order to sail for Dublin, but this route lasted for only a short period of time before it was withdrawn.

The words 'Post Boy' does not refer to age, it was just a

general reference term used at the time, when in fact the majority were men of military or naval experience. The mail was carried in a backpack which was placed over both shoulders and weighed up to 50lbs. in weight. Later the weight was reduced to 30lbs. in order to ease the burden on the horses which accounted for better endurance and speed. The maximum Post Boys were allowed to travel in each 24 hours was 20 miles. This method of post delivery lasted

Post Boy circa 1700

R. Chamber Jones
Bridges and Ferries
Courtesy Dinefwr Press

until the latter part of the 18th century, when the mail coach came into existence.

Over the next century the mail to Ireland steadily increased, besides the Royal dispatches ordinary post from public sources also developed.

In 1572 a weekly crossing for the conveyance of mail began between London and Dublin via Holyhead, using a relay of messengers and horses. The journey was long and treacherous covering roads that were no more than rough tracks. The journey to Holyhead took 29 hours in summer and 41 hours in winter, this required crossing the River Conway and the Menai Straits by ferry. The arrival at the

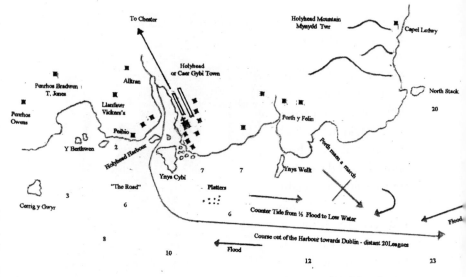

Drawing from a print of Lewis Morris's Map of Holyhead
circa 1750.
(Lewis Morris Customs Official and Hydrographer)
Born Llanfihangel, Anglesey (1701–1765)
Completed Survey of Plans of Harbours, Bars, Bays, and Roads,
in the St George's Channel 1748

Author's collection
D. Lloyd Hughes & D. M. Williams
'The Story of Port' 1981
Courtesy Mrs Sian Murphy

port was followed by the unpredictable crossing of the Irish Sea by barque.

In 1647 a Postmaster General was appointed, and after the restoration of Charles II to the throne an Act of Parliament known as the 'Charter of the Post Office' was passed which instituted the Post office and its statutes which are still relevant today and the Royal Mail as we know it came into existence. In a further Act of 1711 a General Post Office in London and a General Letter Office in Dublin were established.

Holyhead Harbour print of 1785
D. Lloyd Hughes & D. M. Williams
'The Story of Port' 1981
Courtesy Mrs Sian Murphy

Conditions of the road from London to Chester were improved to some extent but generally the state road from Chester to Holyhead remained unchanged. Passenger services to Ireland mainly concentrated on sailing's from Parkgate on the Dee estuary and Liverpool. The Royal Mail however continued to use Holyhead the shorter sea route; in that travelling across land was quicker than by sea.

The road from Chester to Holyhead had major geographical drawbacks. Firstly the crossing of the River Conway by ferry, then the headlands of granite; large outcrops of which were at Penmaen Bach, and Penmaenmawr that reached down to the sea; and finally the ferry crossing at the Menai Straits.

To overcome the problems of the granite headlands, there were three route possibilities. The first from Conway and along the sands around Penmaen Bach and Penmaenmawr and then directly across the Lavan sands to the Beaumaris ferry and Beaumaris, and from there across Anglesey to Holyhead. However tidal conditions dictated this route but it favoured the couriers of the mail as the fastest route. The second, again on the sands around Penmaen Bach then over the stoney and dangerous track at Penmaenmawr with steep cliffs below and the threat of falling rocks from above, from there along the coast road to Bangor. Finally the last route from Conway was on an old pack horse track round the back of Penmaen Bach, through the Sychnant pass, and passing behind Penmaenmawr to join the coast road to Bangor at Llanfairfechan.

At the end of the 17th Century a new road was built lower down from the original track across Penmaenmawr and again at the beginning of the 18th century further improvements were carried out. In 1765 an act for a turn pike road was passed to run from Menai Bridge (Porthaethewy) to Holyhead passing through Llangefni and Bodedern. Further in 1769 a turnpike road was built from Conway to Penmaenmawr via the Sychnant pass, and once more in 1772–1774 further major road improvements across Penmaenmawr designed by Sylvester were implemented. This with a wall on the seaward side and with a defense against falling rocks on the other.

During the early part of the 18th century there were three sailing's each way between Holyhead and Dublin and in 1740 a further additional sailing was introduced. By 1772 there was a daily packet boat sailing (so named after the packets of mail that it carried) now under the auspices of the Post Office. The mail left London every weekday and was due in Dublin on the sixth day. However the Post Office decided to reduce the number of boats in use with the intention of improving the service with better organisation. The Post Master General entered into an agreement with several contractors of packet boats, and their provision was to provide sound and sufficient boats for the conveyance of mails. Five packets of 70tons were provided, named

'Dartmouth', 'Le de Spencer', 'Hillsborough', 'Clermont' and 'Bessborough' which were commanded by Naval officers who had warrants with the Post Office. It was the owners responsibility if the boat became unfit for service to replace it. The sea crossing varied between seventeen hours and two days according to the prevailing weather conditions of wind and tide.

As an aid to safety at sea the Skerries Rock lighthouse, and the South Stack lighthouse, were built and lit on 4th Nov. 1717 and 9th Feb. 1809 respectively.

With the road improvements carried out along the North Wales coast apart from the ferries at Conway and Menai Bridge, the first Royal Mail coach service began in 1785 carrying Irish Mail and passengers to Holyhead, thereby replacing the Post Boys. Leaving from the coaching inn The Golden Cross at Charing Cross in London at 8pm.

South Stack Lighthouse erected 1809
Courtesy Roy Davies

*** **The Royal Mail Coach, London to Holyhead via Chester**
Dep. London   8pm travelling through:
       Northampton 5.25am Stop.   30 minutes for
                                   Breakfast.

Letterworth
Hickley
Atherstone
Tamworth

Lichfield	2pm	Stop.	45 minutes for Dinner.
Stafford	5.5pm	Stop.	15 minutes for Tea
Nantwich			
Chester	12.5am	Stop.	1 hour for Supper
Holywell			
St. Asaph	6.0am	Stop.	20 minutes for Breakfast
Conway	9.35am	Stop.	Ferry crossing 35 minutes
Bangor Ferry	12.40pm	Stop.	1 hour for Dinner (George & Dragon) and Ferry crossing

*** Edward Watson 'Royal Mail to Ireland' 1917

Journey across Anglesey 3hrs. 33min.

Arr. Holyhead 5.13pm (Eagle and Child) Journey time 45hrs. 13 min.

The return departure from Holyhead was at 7am travelling in a similar nature, with the coach scheduled to arrive in London at 4am of the third morning.

Journey time 45hrs.

A telegraph station was erected at Holyhead enabling the approaching packet to signal to the harbour so that the mail coach might be detained if necessary, thereby saving 24 hours' delay to the mail.

Following the inaugural journey of the Royal Mail coach passenger traffic also significantly increased. However facilities for embarking and disembarking passengers were somewhat primitive. The harbour at Holyhead although it had been used for centuries as a port to Ireland with it being the shortest route, it was just a natural sheltered inlet on the

Painting of the 'Eagle and Child' as a 18th Century Coaching Inn,
by Holyhead artist Dr Kenneth Roberts

Courtesy Dr Kenneth Roberts

West coast of Anglesey. It was tidal, the inlet flooded at high tide and was an area of mud and sand at low tide. There was no quayside or landing stage, therefore both passengers and mail were ferried from the shore by small wherries to the awaiting packet boats. At low tide the packets' anchored off Parry's Island which was situated to the south side of the entrance to inlet and embarking passengers had to make a precarious trip across the mud and sand flats on foot to the awaiting wherries with the lucky ones being carried on the backs of sailors.

In 1801 an Act Of Union was passed that brought the United Kingdom into being, which resulted in the Irish Parliament moving to London. This required the Irish Members of Parliament and other government officials to travel to London, thereby significantly increasing passenger traffic, also the Irish Members requested the same comfort in travelling as their Scottish counterparts. The necessity therefore for proper landing facilities at Holyhead was paramount, and John Rennie was asked by parliament to make a report which he presented in 1802. With continuing pressure finally a select committee headed by Henry Brook Parnell recommended that Salt Island (Ynys Halen) an island at the head of the inlet be purchased and a pier constructed from it , also a road be built connecting the coaching inn The Eagle and Child (Later renamed The Royal) with the pier at an overall estimated cost of £68,862. The building of the pier in a East South East direction 1100ft. (338metres) in length commenced in 1810 and was completed in 1821 and became known as The Admiralty Pier. On the other side of the harbour a graving dock was built, estimated at a cost of £12,000, one of the first in Britain, and alongside this a further pier was also built 330ft. (100metres) in length in a Northerly direction. Also constructed on Salt Island was a Custom House, Harbour Office, and a Lighthouse at the end of the pier. The building of the pier enabled ships to moor along side and facilitate the embarking and disembarking of passengers and mails in safety. They were then transported to and from the coaching inn by horse drawn omnibuses.

In Ireland during the 18th century the river channel in Dublin was used for the berthing of the packet boats. In 1796 a harbour was built known as the Pigeon House Dock, and in 1818 this was replaced by the small port of Howth about eight from Dublin on the northern side of Dublin bay although not convenient it remained the mail pier until 1836. During King George IV's visit via Holyhead to Ireland in 1821, Howth was overlooked for the return journey when the landing place of Dunleary ten miles south of Dublin was chosen. At the King's request the name of Dunleary was changed to that of Kingstown, and the government took in hand the construction of a protected refuge there. It was not until 1836 when construction was completed that Howth was abandoned, and Kingstown became the mail packet port. Today it is known as Dun Laoghaire.

At the entrance to the Admiralty Pier at Holyhead a marble arch was erected to commemorate King George's visit on his journey to Ireland.

Although the mail coach was now in service, the route was still long and treacherous and in 1808 after requests by the Post Office to re route the Royal Mail through Shrewsbury to Holyhead to reduce transit times to Ireland, a parliamentary select committee was set up to evaluate the state of the road that existed at that time, and also that of the Chester to Holyhead road. A decision was taken by the committee to appoint Thomas Telford (1757–1834) the eminent Scottish engineer to carry out surveys for both roads. This took eighteen months to complete, after which Telford submitted his plans and recommendations to the committee. Unfortunately due to a lack of urgency by Parliament it was 1815 when The Holyhead Road Commission came into existence that Telford was commissioned to carry out improvements to the Shrewsbury to Holyhead road which came in at an estimated cost of £394,480. Included in the construction were three major projects. One the Waterloo Bridge over the river Conway at Betws-y-coed. Built of cast iron with a span of 105ft. (32mtrs.) and with an inscription that was cast into the side of the bridge which read as follows 'The arch was constructed in the same year that the battle of Waterloo was fought'. Although it was designed and constructed in 1815 it was not erected until 1816. Following this was the building of a new route through the Nan Francon pass in the river Ogwen valley. There was already a road through the pass built in 1802 by Lord Penrhyn, (Sir Richard Pennant) the owner of the Penrhyn slate quarries which was used by private coach contractors between Shrewbury and Holyhead. It was however situated at the bottom of the valley and consequently it required coaches to negotiate steep gradients over the hilly terrain when leaving the pass. Telford therefore chose to ignore this route and planned his road at the side of the pass which involved heavy construction work and blasting of rock. The reasoning being was the keeping of gradients to a constant level throughout the whole length of the road, thereby giving coaches a consistent plane over which to travel in order to maintain a constant speed. The final major undertaking was the design and construction of his masterpiece the Menai Suspension Bridge over the Menai Straits to Anglesey. The world's first modern suspension bridge. The dimensions of which were, length 1,368ft. (417mtrs.), the main span 577ft. (176mtrs.), width 39ft. (12mtrs.). Construction began in 1819 and the bridge opened on the 31st January 1926. Prior to this the old post road across the Isle of Anglesey was in disrepair and dangerous and between 1818 and 1822 Telford built a new toll road across the island from Menai Bridge to Holyhead with an embankment across the Stanley sands (the Valley Cob), also included were toll gates at Llanfair P.G, Nant, Gwalchmai, Caergeiliog, and the Stanley embankment. Telford also turned his attention to improving the road between Conway and Bangor which included building a suspension bridge over the river at Conway at an overall estimated cost of £192,552.

With the road completed from London to Holyhead, the Royal Mail was timed to leave the coaching inn The Swan With Two Necks at Lad Lane in London at 8pm.
*** The Royal Mail coach London to Holyhead via Shrewsbury

Dep. London 8pm travelling through:

Barnet
Colney
St. Albans
+ Redburn   10.44pm Distance 24m. 3f.
Market St.
Dunstable
+ Brickhill   12.32am =   17m. 7f.
Fenny Stratford
Stoney Stratford 1.26am
+ Towcester   2.12am =   16m. 6f.
+ Daventry   3.25am   12m. 2f.
+ Dunchurch   4.11am =   7m. 6f.
+ Coventry   5.18am =   11m. 2f.
Stonebridge   6.07am
+ Birmingham   7.08am =   18m. 2f. 35minutes
                                          allowed
+ Wednesbury   8.29am =   7m. 7f.
Bilston
+ Wolverhamton   9.01am =   5m. 3f.
Shiffnal   10.14am

*** + Haygate   10.59am =   20m 2f. Bags dropped
                                          here and taken up from
                                          Wellington.
Shrewsbury   11.59am   5 minutes allowed.
+ Nescliffe   12.52pm   18m. 6f.
+ Oswestry   1.45pm   9m. 4f.
Chirk
+ Llangollen   2.57pm   12m. 4f.
Corwen   3.57pm   28 minutes allowed.
+ Tynant   5.01pm   16m. 4f.
Cernioge   5.39pm

+ New Stables	6.21pm	14m.
Capel Curig	7.02pm	
+ Tynamus	7.46pm	14m. 6f. 5 minutes allowed (Penryn Arms)
+ Bangor Ferry	8.43pm	8m. 6f.
+ Mona Inn	9.43pm	10m.

Journey time across Anglesey 2hrs. 12min.
Arr. Holyhead   10.55pm (Eagle and Child)
Journey time 26hrs. 55min. 259m. 2f.
 + Change of horses. "f" furlong.   (220yds.) (.125m.)

*** Edward Watson 'Royal Mail to Ireland'

The return departure from Holyhead was at 4.15am and covered the same route and destinations and was scheduled to arrive the next morning at 6.54am.
Journey time 26hrs. 39mins.

In Spring of 1819 the New Steam Packet Co. informed the Post Master General that they were going to establish a packet station at Holyhead and offered the Post Office their two ships the *S.S.Ivanhoe* and *S.S.Talbot* to carry the mail. The Post Office did not want to relinquish their monopoly on the mail which they had held for centuries to another company and in 1821 the Post Office in its own right brought into service two steam paddle ships the Meteor and the Lightning thus reducing the time for crossing the Irish Channel to 8 hrs. Eventually due to the Act of Union the mail packet route came under the authority of the Admiralty.

However the age of steam was now at hand and the Railway Era had arrived. Within 22yrs. of the opening of Telford's Menai Bridge the Irish Mail Train came into service.

To bring into perspective the cost of projects incurred in the 19th Century to that which is relevant today, i.e. £1000 of expenditure is equivalent to approximately £89,000 of present day value.

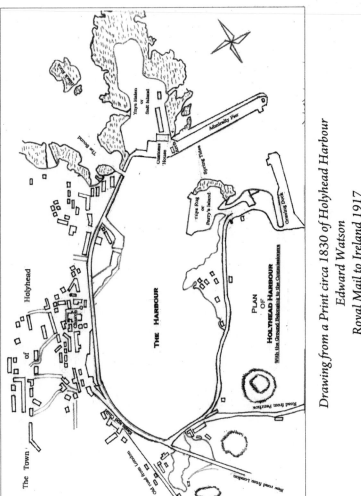

Drawing from a Print circa 1830 of Holyhead Harbour
Edward Watson
Royal Mail to Ireland 1917   *Author Collection*

Chapter 2

The age of Steam and the Arrival of the Railways

The age of steam began not on the railways but in the Cornish Tin and Copper mines where steam engines were used to pump water from the mines. Thomas Newcomen (1663–1729) the English inventor patented in 1705 one of the first steam engines to be put to practical use in a industrial setting. It was however James Watt (1736–1819) always associated with the age of steam that made improvements to the Newcomen engine that set the pace for the Industrial Revolution. In 1763 he repaired a Newcomen engine belonging to John Anderson and found it inefficient and wasteful of fuel. Watt realised that by condensing steam in a separate tank, a condenser, he could make the engine more efficient and safer, also having applied Joseph Black (1728–1790) the Scottish chemist's properties on the discovery of latent heat. In 1774 Watt entered into partnership with Mathew Boulton the industrialist to produce steam engines and through research patents were taken out for a rotary engine. Steam power by now had moved into the cotton and woollen mills replacing water driven machinery. By 1788 marine propulsion also had became a possibility. Watt also defined the unit of one horse power, the rate at which work is done when 33,000lbs are raised in one minute, and the watt as a unit of electricity is named after him today.

Richard Trevithick (1771–1833)

The first development of a locomotive was by Richard Trevithick at Coalbrookdale in Shropshire although there is doubt that this engine was ever in use. Never the less Trevithick in 1804 produced a locomotive for the Penydarren ironworks in Merthyr Tydfil to transport iron to the Merthyr-Cardiff canal. On the 21st February 1804 the engine aptly named 'Penydarren' hauled a train of five wagons carrying ten tons of iron on the 9 mile (14.4km) journey at a speed of 5mph (8kph). This was the first steam engine to run on rails. Unfortunately the Penydarren only made three journeys as each time the 7ton engine broke the cast iron rails. Samuel Homfray the owner of the works came to the conclusion that it was unlikely to reduce his running costs so he abandoned the project.

However Tevithick's locomotive had one important feature the turning of the exhaust steam up the chimney, producing a draft which drew hot gases from the fire more powerfully through the boiler.

The early development of the first locomotives was solely about transporting coal and other minerals and it was not until the opening of the Stockton-Darlington Railway that the idea of carrying passengers on a commercial basis came into being.

George Stephenson (1781–1848)

George Stephenson engineer and locomotive designer in his early years became engineman at Dewley colliery and then at the age of twenty seven found employment at Killingworth colliery. Where during his spare time he took engines apart to understand how they were constructed, including engines built by Newcomen and Watt. By 1812 he was promoted to engine wright. In 1813 he became aware of William Hedley, Timothy Hackworth, and Jonathan Forster's attempts to build a locomotive at Wylam colliery called the 'Puffing Billy' and by 1814 Stephenson had constructed a locomotive which was called 'Blutcher'. The engine had two vertical cylinders let into the boiler, the pistons of which drove the gears. It was capable of pulling thirty tons up a gradient at 4mph (6.4kph). Unlike most other engines at that time which were driven by rack pinions for progression Stephenson's engine had flanged wheels, Further improvements to the engine were made in 1815 that allowed the connecting rods to drive the wheels directly. Over the next five years Stephenson built sixteen engines at Killingworth. Impressed by his work the owners at the colliery in 1819 gave him the task of building an 8 mile (12.8km) railway from Hetton to the river Wear at Sunderland. He constructed a locomotive named the Hetton Colliery No. 1 and this engine worked continuously at the colliery until 1908. Later in 1925 it led under its own steam the Railway Centenary Cavalcade.

Edward Pease a former wool merchant could visualise the need for a railroad to carry coal from the collieries at Darlington to the port at Stockton. His vision was for horses to pull wagons by rail. Pease and a group of business colleagues proposed the forming of a railway between the Stockton and Darlington and on the 19th April 1821 an act of parliament was passed to build a horse railway along this route. Stephenson arranged a meeting with Pease and suggested he should consider a locomotive railway for the project, stating that an engine could pull ten tons for one ton pulled by horses. Stephenson invited Pease to Killingworth colliery to see his engine Blutcher at work, impressed by what he saw Pease offered Stephenson the post of Chief Engineer of the Stockton and Darlington railway. Pease then applied to parliament to have a clause added to the Act of 1821 for the allowance to make and erect locomotives or moveable engines.

Stephenson working with William Loch had patented their own make of cast iron rails, however he turned to John

Birkenshaw an engineer at Bedlinton ironworks who had perfected a method of rolling wrought iron rails in fifteen feet lengths which were superior to the ones he and Loch were making. Although more costly Stephenson decided to use Birkenshaw's rails for the Stockton and Darlington Railway.

In 1824 Edward Pease, Michael Longbridge, George Stephenson, and his son Robert born 1803 formed a company to build locomotives. The company was called the Robert Stephenson & Co. of Newcastle-upon-Tyne, the first in the world to build locomotives. Recruited to the company was Timothy Hackworth who with William Hedley had produced the Puffing Billy. The first locomotive built was in1825 called 'Active' but it was later changed to 'Locomotion'. It had a single fire tube and two vertical cylinders let into the boiler and four wheels coupled by rods.

The Stockton and Darlington railway opened on the 29th September 1825. The train consisted of Locomotion and tender driven by George Stephenson, six wagons loaded with coals and flour, a coach for carrying dignitaries and officials of the railway, twenty one wagons fitted out for passengers, plus a further six wagons of coal, in all a train of thirty six vehicles. The journey of 9 miles (14.4km)took two hours averaging 8mph (12.8kph), during the final descent into Stockton a speed of 15mph (24kph) was achieved.

In 1828 the boiler of Locomotion exploded killing the driver, the problem being the inability to produce enough steam for a twenty mile run. It was rebuilt by Timothy Hackworth who put in an enlarged boiler and a return fire tube. This rectified the problem and improved performance, however it was replaced in 1827 by Hackworth's 'Royal George', a locomotive with six wheels, its cylinders were vertical and inverted and on the outside of the boiler and the connecting rods drove the rear wheels.

Locomotion went down in history as the first railway steam engine to pull a passenger train.

The Liverpool and Manchester railway was founded on the 24th May 1823. It was set up by Henry Booth its secretary and treasurer and merchants from Liverpool and Manchester and a bill was laid before parliament in 1825 but was rejected through inaccuracies in the surveying of the line. In 1826 a second Bill was presented to parliament which was passed. The line opened on the 15th September 1830 the first inter city passenger railway in which all trains were timetabled. Prior to the opening the Directors were unsure whether to use locomotives or stationary engines on the line. In order to come to a conclusion a decision was taken to hold a competition at Rainhill known as the 'Rainhill Trials' offering a prize of £500 to the winner. The criteria for the competition was that each competing engine had to haul a load three times its own weight at 10mph (16kph) and complete twenty journeys up and down the track at Rainhill roughly the equivalent to the distance between Liverpool and Manchester. Ten locomotives were originally entered but only five turned up for the trials and of these two were withdrawn because of mechanical problems. Of the others 'Sans Pariel' and 'Novelty' did reasonably well over two days of the trials but by the third day only 'Rocket' was left in the competition. The Rocket completed the final trial covering 35 miles (56km) in three hours and twelve minutes, Hauling thirteen tons of loaded wagons averaging a speed of 12mph (19.2kph). Rocket on one trip obtained a speed of 25mph (40kph) and as a light engine 29mph (46.4kph) was achieved. The judges awarded the £500 prize to the owners of the Rocket, Robert Stephenson & Co.of Newcastle, and also contracted them to produce locomotives for the railway.

The Rocket had been modified before the competition

the twelve inch diameter iron fire tube was replaced by several two inch multi tubes of copper. This resulted in all the flame and heated air to pass through these tubes to increase very rapidly the area for heating water thereby giving the boiler the ability to generate steam for supplying the cylinders more quickly consequently increasing the speed of the engine. Another beneficial alteration made was that the cylinders coupled to the front pair of wheels were positioned at a thirty five degree angle as from being vertical.

Later in 1830 further modifications were made, a smoke box was added and the chimney shortened, and a further reduction in the angle of the cylinders from thirty five degrees to eight made for a more stable ride. The modified Rocket remained in service on the Liverpool and Manchester line until the late 1830's.

Although not the ultimate in steam locomotion, Rocket laid down the principles and arrangements for future construction of locomotives.

'Pennydarren' 0-4-0
Built by Richard Trevithick in 1804
for the Pennydarren Ironworks in Merthyr Tydfil South Wales
Publishers own print

Chapter 3

Laying the Line Euston to Holyhead
The London and Birmingham Railway

The London and Birmingham Railway was one of the earliest railways in the country and the first one to be built out from London. The line was 112 miles (179km) long and extended from London Euston to Birmingham Curzon St.

As early as 1820 proposals for a railway between London and Birmingham were projected by William Jones however the scheme remained unsupported. In January 1824 the first survey to be carried out for a possible line was made by John Rennie who proposed a route via Oxford and Banbury only by the time he had completed his report in 1826 interest in the project had waned. By 1829 interest again had arisen in the scheme, and Francis Giles carried out a survey proposing a line through Coventry. Initially the two companies that had instigated the Rennie and Giles' surveys issued their own prospectuses separately but were unsuccessful in their endeavours. In 1830 the two rival companies combined their efforts and further surveys by Robert Stephenson in 1830 and 1831 were carried out and the route via Coventry was preferred. The Bill for the London Birmingham Rly. went into the committee stage in Parliament from 5th to 13th April and 21st May to 5th June 1832 where it was passed by the House of Commons after a very vigourous fight. It was then presented to the House of Lords on July 10th 1832 where it was defeated, opposition having come from landowners who feared their privacy and idyllic lifestyle would be compromised by the railway crossing their estates. Also there was reluctance to the bill from those with road and canal interests who could foresee a possible decline in the commercial use of their assets. After a payment of a vast amount of money totaling £700,000 in recompense and enticement to the opposition, and further slight modifications to the plans the Bill for London & Birmingham Rly. was represented to the House of Commons and was passed on 15th March 1833 and in the House of Lords on 22nd April 1833, and given Royal Assent on 6th May 1833.

On 9th September 1833 Robert Stephenson was appointed Chief Engineer for the whole line on a salary of £2000. The original estimate for the railway was £2,500,000, this was to be raised in shares and a further £835,000 in loans. The first contracts were awarded in May 1834 and in all thirty contracts for the line were awarded with some firms having more than one contract. A work force of 12,000 was employed and the average wage for a navvy was three shillings (15p) per day, slightly more than the agricultural wage at the time. The average working day was twenty hours, with two shifts working ten hours.

The line was built throughout with gradients no steeper than 1in 330 per mile, apart for the mile from Euston to Camden which included a stretch of 1in 66. The construction of the 112mile (179km) line required 6 viaducts 300 bridges and 7 tunnels, three of which were extremly long. The formation of cuttings and embankments realised the removing of 16,000,000 cubic metre's of material.

The Tunnels

Primrose Hill Tunnel 1,164yds. (1060mtrs.)
Initial excavations was through clay which required a pickaxe to cut it, but as the clay became moist it turned to

soft mud which filled the whole of the excavations and the enormous pressure of the clay squeezed mortar out of the joints between the brick lining. To overcome the problem the hardest possible brick had to be used, due to the fact that the original brick used crushed under the immense pressure of the clay, also Roman cement was substituted instead of mortar. The original plan of an 18inch. (45cm) lining had to be increased to 30inch. (75cm) in places. The maximum length of excavation that could be made was 9ft. (2.7mtrs.) before the lining had to be built. This caused the cost of the tunnel to escalate to £160,000.

Watford Tunnel 1792yds. (1633mtrs.)
The Watford tunnel had treacherous pockets of unstable gravel and sand within the chalk sub strata which could burst into the workings without warning. One such incident resulted in tragedy when an inrush caused ten men to be enveloped in the deluge.

Kilsby Tunnel 2442yds. (2226mtrs.)
The Kilsby Tunnel was extremly dangerous and difficult piece of construction. The fact being that quicksand bogged with water occupied a quarter of the tunnels length. To drain water from this section took pumping engines nine months to clear at an average of 2000 gallons per minute before tunneling could begin on this part. In all eighteen working shafts were sunk to speed excavation and 1300 men were constantly employed on this project. On completion two ventilation shafts of 60 ft. diameter had been built; the largest being 130ft. deep and used one million bricks. The quantity of material excavated was over 1777,000 cubic mtrs. and 30 million bricks were used on the lining of the tunnel.

North Church Tunnel 345yds.(315mtrs.)

Linslade Tunnel 285yds. (260mtrs.)

Stowe Hill Tunnel 484yds. (441mtrs.)

Beechwood Tunnel 292yds. (266mtrs.)

Major Construction Works

Miles	Station
0	Euston
1	Camden Town Depot – Retaining Walls and Primrose Hill Tunnel
18	Watford – Watford Embankment, Colne Viaduct, Watford Tunnel
32	Tring – Tring Cutting
48	Denbigh Hall
52	Wolverton – Wolverton Embankment and Viaduct
63	Blisworth – Blisworth Cutting
70	Weedon
79	– Kilsby Tunnel
83	Rugby,
	– Avon viaduct
94	Coventry
	– Beechwood Tunnel
112	Birmingham – Rea Viaduct

The stations along the line were designed by George Aitchison, whilst the two impressive termini buildings at Euston and Curzon St. were designed by Phillip Hardwick. The famous edifice the Greek Doric Arch or propylaeum at Euston being the outstanding feature. In all there were eight major and seventeen intermediate stations.

Stations

EUSTON	Cheddington	Brandon
WILLESDEN Jct.	Leighton Buzzard	COVENTRY
Harrow	BLETCHLEY	Berkswell
Bushy	WOLVERTON	Hampton
WATFORD Jct.	Castlethorpe	Marston Green
Kings Langley	Blisworth	Stetchford
Boxmoor	Weedon	BIRMINGHAM
Berkhamstead	Welton	
Tring.	RUGBY	

Initially the locomotives used for the line, the Bury 0-4-0 were somewhat deficient in power and unable to make the gradient out of Euston under their own steam. To compensate for the lack of power stationary engines had to be provided and sighted at Camden to haul the trains by cable up the gradient. Contact between Euston and Camden was by pneumatic telegraph which sounded a whistle to signal the movement of trains. This was later replaced by electric telegraph. Amongst the railway committee were two directors Messrs. Rathbone and Cropper who were ever critical of Robert Stephenson having previously had altercations with his father George whilst the Liverpool and Manchester Rly. was being built, and it was on their insistence that Edward Bury was to supply the locomotives. If Robert Stephenson and Co. of Newcastle, locomotive builders had been allowed to provide locomotives from the outset then the need for cable hauled assistance would never have been required. It was 1844 before locomotives were introduced on the line capable of making the gradient under their own steam.

By 9th April 1838 a section of the line from Euston to a temporary station at Denbigh Hall 48 miles (77km) distant, and a further section of line of 29 miles (46km) from Rugby to Birmingham were ready for use. In the meantime until the Kilsby Tunnel and Blisworth Cutting were completed, a stage coach service operated from Denbigh Hall to Rugby to connect both sections of track. The line was finally completed on 15th September 1838 only three and a half months over the anticipated four years. The overall cost was £5,5000,000, which included £350,000 for locomotives and rolling stock. The official opening was on 17th September 1838 when a train carrying directors and shareholders travelled the whole route pulled by locomotive 'Harvey Combe' with Robert Stephenson travelling on the footplate.

Entrance to Euston Station circa 1838
Courtesy J. Addyman & V. Howorth
'Robert Stephenson Railway Engineer'

The Grand Junction Railway

As early as 1823 influential business men from Liverpool and Birmingham joined forces to form a committee and to develop plans for a railway from Liverpool to Birmingham seeing the potential for trade between the port and the industrial Midlands. The company was known as the Birmingham and Liverpool Railroad Co. Plans were drawn up for a line from Birmingham to Birkenhead and a submission to Parliament was made. However there was opposition from those with other interests, namely landowners and canal companies and the scheme failed.

In 1830 when the Liverpool and Manchester Railway was opened, and enthusiasm in the country for this mode of transport was ever increasing the Birmingham and Liverpool Railroad Co. was revived. The majority of the directors were Liverpool financiers that were part of the L & M and three engineers George Stephenson, Joseph Locke, and John Urpeth Rastrick, who had all worked on that line were engaged by the company. A Decision was taken to route the proposed railway from Liverpool and not Birkenhead. This required crossing the River Mersey and in consequence the line had to be routed to where this was possible. In 1831 a spur almost 5 miles (8km) long on the L & M line had been opened at Newton Junction to provide a link with Warrington. It was therefore decided to plan the proposed railway from Warrington to Birmingham, and a prospectous was issued to what was to become the Grand Junction Railway. Using this route via the L & M not only resolved the problem of the Mersey crossing, but also opened a way for Manchester to connect with Midlands. George Stephenson was appointed as Chief Engineer on a salary of £2000 whilst Joseph Locke and John Rastrick were appointed his assistants.

This time with careful planning and preparation, and with suitable remuneration's to the opposition of land owners and canal companies a Bill for the Grand Junction Railway was presented to Parliament, where it was speedily passed by both the House of Commons and Lords. It received the Royal Assent on 6th May 1833, the same day as the London and Birmingham Rly.

Although Joseph Locke was fully committed to the construction of the line, John Rastrick however was engaged in other projects which were taking up much of his time. This caused friction with the Company Directors which eventually led to his resignation in September 1833. After Rastrick had left, engineering was shared on an equal status by Stephenson and Locke, something that Stephenson reluctantly accepted due to Locke having been his understudy on the L & M Over the next two years Locke undertook the northern section of the line from Whitmore to Warrington whilst Stephenson concentrated south from Whitmore to Birmingham. Relations between the two engineers deteriorated somewhat further and with Stephenson involved with other commitments he also resigned from the company on September 16th 1835. This led to Locke taking overall control of construction with an increase in salary to £1200.

Construction was initiated on 22nd May 1833 by the Board of Directors, and one of the objectives of the Grand Junction Rly. was to take over the five mile line from Newton Junction to Warrington. The Directors of which. realising the potential of their little line held the G.J.R. to ransom by demanding a higher price for their shares, £125 for each £100 held, as well as a settlement of outstanding £20,000 of debts. The directors of the G.J.R. were disappointed by the N. & W demands in that they made a survey for another line to counter them.. This line was to run from Moore to Colliers Green and cross the Mersey at Fiddlers Ferry just west of Newton. This move took the N. & W. shareholders by surprise and they accepted the G.J.R.'s offer for shares at face value, plus an offer to pay £15,503 of their debts. The total purchase price paid for the line was £73,400 and a further £6,000 was required to upgrade the track.

The line from Newton Junction to Birmingham Curzon St. was 82 miles (131km) long and the estimated cost of construction from Warrington to Birmingham 77 miles (123km) was in the region of £20,000 per mile. In all seven major stations and nineteen intermediate stations were built along the line.

Stations

Newton Junction	Madeley	James Bridge
WARRINGTON	WHITMORE	Bescot Bridge
Moore	Norton Bridge	Newton Road
Preston Brook	Bridgeford	Perry Bar
Acton	STAFFORD	BIRMINGHAM
HARTFORD	Penkridge	
Winsford	Spread Eagle	
Minshull Vernon	Four Ashes	
Coppenhall	WOLVERHAMTON	
CREWE	Willenhall	
Basford Hall		

At Birmingham a temporary station at Vauxhall had to be built due to the new station at Curzon St. not being completed in time before the line opened. A further problem presented itself on the approach to Birmingham the line routed from Perry Bar to Vauxhall went via Aston Park and the resident at Aston Hall, James Watt jnr., son of the famous engineer was bitterly opposed to the line running so close to his land, to the extent that he spent £2,000 on legal fees to resist any development there. Locke planned a detour which required a further Act of Parliament, and the proposed new route of the line necessitated the building of several bridges and a viaduct at

Aston. However construction for the whole line was completed in the record time of four years and two months and came in on budget at a cost of £1,470,000.

Major Construction Works

Miles	Station
0	Newton Junction
5	Warrington

Warrington Viaduct crossing the River Mersey and Irwell and Mersey canal.

Preston Brook, Aqueduct and Cutting.

Dutton Viaduct crossing the River Weaver, and Duke of Bridgewaters' canal (20 arches of 65ft. span) cost £54,440.

17	Hartford

Vale Royal Viaduct, crossing the River Weaver (5 arches of 63ft. span) Hartford Cutting.

29	Crewe
40	Whitmore
54	Stafford

Penkridge Viaduct over the River Penk, cost £6,000.

Hampstead Cutting, cost £66,673.

69	Wolverhampton
82	Birmingham

Aston Viaduct over Lichfield Rd. and Birmingham and Fazely Canal.

Birmingham Viaduct crossing Lawley St. and River Rea.

The Grand Junction Railway opened on 4th July 1837, but prior to the official opening the Board of Directors decided on 24th June 1837 to make their own through journey to Birmingham. A train of three coaches and a mail coach left Liverpool at 6/30am pulled by locomotive 'Doctor Dalton' an engine built by Sharpe and Roberts & Co. of Manchester. A similar train left Manchester and at Newton Junction both trains were coupled together to continue the journey to Birmingham arriving at 11/30am. On the 4th July 1837 the inaugural train left Vauxhall station in Birmingham at 7am with 'Wildfire' a 2-2-2 engine with 5ft. (152cm) diameter driving wheels built by Robert Stephenson & Co. pulling a train of eight carriages. At Warrington the train divided into two, the first portion went on to Liverpool, whilst a waiting engine took the second part to Manchester. Both destinations were reached at 11/30am. The 97mile (155km) journey having taken four and a half hours at an average speed of about 22m.p.h. (35kmph).

When Curzon St. station opened the platforms for the Great Junction Railway were adjacent to those of the London & Birmingham Railway, thereby giving through access to London from the North.

It was on this railway by the proposal of the post office in January 1838 that the first sorting of mail en route was done, the mail being sorted in a converted horse box. Later specialised 'Mail' coaches were introduced that had the means of dispatching and picking up mail bags at speed without stopping the train.

Crewe Junction
In the early planning of the Grand Junction Railway the line routed by Joseph Locke was to go via Nantwich four miles (6.4km) west of Crewe which was strategically placed as the centre of road and canal systems for South Cheshire with

links to the Potteries, Chester, North Wales and Shropshire. The final plans however avoided Nantwich and a more direct route across the Cheshire plain almost empty of population apart from small settlements of farming communities. The likely reason for the Nantwich route not being chosen was the ever present objections from landowners and canal owners. Another feature was the price of land, with agricultural land being of a lower cost to that of an urban area.

Crewe was only a small hamlet at this time and the main landowner was the Earl of Crewe whose family seat was at Crewe Hall, a mansion built in the 17th Century and after a disastrous fire in 1866 it was rebuilt by Edward Barry. The mansion was just east of the proposed line hence the station was given the name Crewe. The station was built in the parish of Monks Coppenhall, in between Coppenhall to the north and Basford Hall to the south. The station although it was modestly built at first is was classed as a First Class station by the G.J.R., with the probability in mind for it to be a junction and a hub in the railway system, connecting the North, Manchester, Chester, Birkenhead, and the Potteries with main line.

The first of these connections was the Chester to Crewe Railway Co. line which was taken over by the G.J.R. and opened on 1 October 1840. Two years later the Manchester South Union Railway who sought a line from Manchester south to Rugby to give a more direct route to London, finally due to financial restraints and amendments to the Act of Parliament it amalgamated with the Manchester Cheshire and Staffordshire Railway to become the Manchester and Birmingham Railway, and a warrant was given to build a line 30¾ miles (49km) from Manchester to Crewe via Stockport, Wilmslow, and Sandbach, to join the G.J.R. at Crewe.

With the opening of the Crewe to Chester Rly. a decision was made by the G.J.R. in June 1840 to move its engineering works for the repair, maintenance of engines, and rolling stock, also the building of locomotives from its works in Edge Hill in Liverpool to Crewe thereby giving it a more direct route to the main line. The position chosen for sighting the works was north of the junction in between the Warrington and Chester lines. To house the workforce required, and the company management, the town of Crewe was created. The contract for the construction of the works and the building of two hundred houses for the employees which began in 1841 was given to a firm of Liverpool builders. By 1842 the population of the town had reached one thousand, and further developments of houses, schools, community halls, and a temporary church saw a further increase in the population to two thousand in 1843. The works covering seven acres of land opened in December 1843, and the first church 'Christ Church' in Prince Albert St. was consecrated in 1845.

In 1843 Lord Crewe built the Crewe Arms Hotel adjacent to the station, the first purpose built railway hotel in the country, and is still in use up to the present day. In 1864 the hotel was leased to the London and North Western Railway Co. who eventually bought it in 1877. One notable visitor to the Crewe Arms Hotel in 1848 was Queen Victoria and Prince Albert who with their retinue of thirty staff made an unscheduled stop at the town on their way back from Scotland and were accommodated in the hotel.

Due to increase in traffic major reconstruction to the station was carried out in 1861 along with enlargements to the works and the town. Further improvements were again made in 1896 and 1906, and by this time one thousand passenger and freight trains were either stopping or passing through Crewe Junction within a twenty four hour period.

The Chester and Crewe Railway

In 1826 George Stephenson surveyed for a line 20½ miles (33km) in length linking Chester and Crewe across the Cheshire plain but it never came into fruition. It was to be another decade before Stephenson again surveyed the route acting on behalf of Chester and Cheshire businessmen. Several routes were considered, one the shortest was to join the Grand Junction Railway at the Vale Royal viaduct over the River Weaver, however it had its drawbacks in that severe engineering works and stiff gradients would be required to traverse Delamere Forest, therefore a less demanding route although longer was proposed. An Act of Parliament for the railway was passed and the Royal Assent given on 30 June 1837. The estimated cost of construction was £250,000.

Robert Stephenson was appointed as engineer, and Thomas Brassey a twenty nine year old from Buerton Cheshire was appointed contractor. He had already worked for the G.J.R. as a contractor building the Penkridge Viaduct.

By 1839 although the line was reasonably level and with only a low eight arch viaduct being the only major piece of engineering work which was required to cross the River Weaver at Worleston near Nantwich, estimates were exceeded which led to financial difficulties for the company. The Directors of the line approached the G.J.R. who incorporated the company after an Act of Parliament on the 19th May 1840, even with the Chester and Crewe Railway never having operated a train on the line.. The railway was completed, and finally opened on 1st October 1840.

Stations

CREWE	Tattenhall Rd
Worleston	Waverton
Calveley	CHESTER
Beeston Castle	

The line not only linked Chester with Crewe but also provided a link to Mersyside by joining at Chester, the Chester and Birkenhead Railway which opened on 23rd September 1840. This gave a route for the Post Office to dispatch the Irish Mails by packet boat via Birkenhead which began on 6th April 1841.

The Chester and Holyhead Railway
The final link between London, Holyhead and Dublin was the creation of the Chester and Holyhead Railway, which linked up with the Crewe and Chester Railway (then owned by the Great Junction Railway).

It was however ten years from the mid 1830s, with various schemes and surveys put forward for a final rail link from London that a decision was made on the North Wales section of track. If the Menai Straits had not been such an obstacle then Holyhead already a packet port for Dublin would have been chosen from the beginning, being the shortest sea route to Ireland. Consequently other alternatives for rail links and ports were put forward, namely Porth Dinllaen on the Lleyn peninsular and Ormes Bay (Llandudno).

Henry Archer manager of the Ffestiniog Railway proposed at a meeting in Dublin on the 9th August 1835 for a packet port to be built at Porth Dinllaen and from there a rail link to London. In 1836 Charles Vignoles (who had surveyed the Liverpool and Manchester Railway) was brought in to survey possible routes to London through the mountains.

His first survey was via Tremadoc, Ffestiniog, Bala, Llangollen, Shrewsbury, Iron Bridge, and Wolverhampton a distance from London of 244 miles (390km) There was however steep gradients to address some of up to 1 in 16, also a tunnel of 2 miles (3.2km) length under the Pass of

Treweryd. His second survey was through Barmouth, Towyn, Machynllech, Dinas Mawddwy, and Llanfair to join up at Shrewsbury. Gradients were again a problem, and the line required a 3 mile (4.8km) tunnel under the Pass of Bwlch Fedwen. A third survey for a route via east of Machynllech, Newtown, Snead, Bishops Castle, Ludlow, Worcester, and Oxford giving a distance to London of 260 miles (416km). Once more gradients were a problem, with another requirement for a tunnel 1½ miles in length under the Carno Pass. A fourth route a more viable one was recommended by Vignoles for a route through Barmouth, Bala, and Llangollen with a principal gradient of 1 in 150 to join the trial line to Wolverhampton. The estimated costs of these mountainous routes was £3½ million. Finally Vignoles was asked to survey a route from Chester to Holyhead and from Bangor to Porth Dinllaen. The former he stated would require crossing the Menai Straits which in his opinion was to great a project to be reflected on. The latter he thought would be expensive, requiring four tunnels and as many viaducts.

The other alternative to Holyhead was Ormes Bay proposed by the engineer John Jenkins. This was for the building of a breakwater and harbour between the Great and Little Ormes at a cost of £200,000, and a rail link along the North Wales coast to Crewe by passing Chester at a cost of £600,000. In 1837 the Ormes Bay or St. Georges Harbour Railway as it was known presented a Bill before Parliament but was unsuccessful in its application. The reason being that Ormes Bay is 96 miles (153km) from Dublin, against 70 miles (112km) from Porth Dinllaen and 62 miles (99km) from Holyhead and the speed of mails being the priority of the Post Office and Government, in that travelling across land was quicker by land than by sea.

Between 1838 and 1842 attempts were made to approve

a line to Holyhead. Francis Giles the eminent engineer had made a survey for a proposed line between Chester and Holyhead. He envisaged a new bridge at Conway and that Telford's bridge across the Menai Straits be used for trains. This required locomotives at each end of the bridge detaching their coaches and then for the coaches to be hauled across the bridge by ropes attached to stationary engines. George Stephenson at a meeting of the Chester and Crewe Railway Co. on the 14th November 1838 supported Giles in his survey. He was then asked to make his own survey as a second opinion, again coming out in favour of a line to Holyhead, with the same principal of Giles' in crossing the Menai Straits. Stephenson also commented on Vignoles' line via Bala as impracticable.

Two Admiralty surveys were carried out in 1838, one by Lt. W. L. Sheringham who came down in favour of Porth Dinllaen, whilst the other by Capt. Beaufort (of the Beaufort Scale for wind velocity) recommended Holyhead as already having harbour facilities. Commissioners appointed by the government on 30th December 1840 left London to inspect the various schemes that were made by Vignoles, Giles, and Stephenson and from evidence that was gathered they came down in favour of the North Wales coast route. Adding to this a further Admiralty survey by Rear Admiral Sir James Gordon, and Capt. Beechey recommended Holyhead as the most suitable port. It was not until 1842 that a select committee of the House of Commons was set up to question Post Office communications with Ireland, and through their deliberations Holyhead was again preferred to Porth Dinllaen. Further support for Holyhead came by another third Admiralty survey, and also in a survey by James Walker the civil engineer. Walker also having examined the Chester and Holyhead railway route proposed in his report to the commissioners that a separate bridge be built across the Menai Straits in preference to Giles' and Stephensons' use of Telfords' bridge. Stephenson therefore changed his previous proposal and recommended construction of a new bridge to be sighted using the Britannia rock in the Straits.

In March 1839 a prospectus for the Great Holyhead Railway backed by the Chester and Crewe railway was published. It was however further four years on the 10th November 1843 that the promoters of the Chester and Holyhead Railway published their intention to apply for an Act of Incorporation. The Board of Directors consisted of nine members that were on the board of the London and Birmingham Railway, three that were board members of the Chester and Birkenhead Railway and six others. In February 1844 William Rockford Collett was made chairman, and Robert Stephenson was appointed as engineer. His father due to some disagreement had withdrawn his services.

Finally a Bill was presented to Parliament by Owen Stanley M.P. on behalf of the Chester and Holyhead Railway Co. and was read for the first time on 14th March 1844 and received Royal Assent on the 4th July 1844. However their was one exclusion from the Bill that being the section of line from the West bank of the River Ogwen and across the Menai Straits to Llanfair P.G. as this would need further surveying. A Bill for this section was introduced at a later date and eventually on the 30th June 1845 Royal Assent was given. It was to Stephensons' advantage that the original Bill of 1844 was passed as this gave him extra engineering time, instead of waiting a further twelve months for the lines full approval. The incorporated cost to the Chester and Holyhead Railway Co. for the construction of the line was £2,100,000 for which they were authorised to issue £50 shares and also there was a likelihood of the London and Birmingham Railway contributing £1,000,000.

Fourteen contracts were awarded for the construction of the line 84 miles in length most of which was difficult engineering. Construction began on St. David's' Day 1st March 1845 at the Conway tunnel and by November 5000 men and 500 horses and drivers were employed, by August 1846 the number had increased to 12,388 men 861 horses and drivers. The work involved building bridges, viaducts and sea walls, blasting through tunnels, digging cuttings and forming embankments.

Major Construction Works

Miles	Station	
0	CHESTER	Northgate Tunnel 475yds. (432m)
		Chester Viaduct (45 arches)
		Dee Bridge (Three spans of 98ft. (30m)
		(See Chapter 4)
7	Queensferry	
		Radcliffe Hall Tunnel
12	Flint	Timber Viaduct
16	Holywell	
20	Mostyn Quay	
30	Rhyl	
		Foryd Bridge
34	Abergele	
		Llandulas Viaduct
		Penmaenrhos Tunnel 485yds. (441m)
40	Colwyn Bay	
		Conway Tubular Bridge (See Chapter 4)
		Conway Tunnel 90yds. (82m)

45	Conway	
		Penmaenbach Tunnel 718yds. (654m)
		Penmaenmawr Tunnel 254yds. (231m)
		Viaduct183yds.(169m) 13 spans of 36ft. cast iron girders on ashlar piers. Sea Wall.
		Avalanche Shelter 265yds. (241m)
		Ogwen Viaduct 22arches, 42ft. high 246yds. (224m)
55	Aber	
		River Cregyn viaduct 7 arches 57ft. high
		132yds. (120m)
		Llandgai Tunnel 505yds. (460m)
		Bangor Tunnel 890yds. (810m)
60	Bangor	
		Belmont Tunnel 726yds. (661m)
61½	Menai Bridge	
		Britannia Bridge (See chapter 4)
63	Llanfair P.G.	
		Malltreath Viaduct 19 arches
		Bodorgan No. 1 Tunnel 413yds. (378m)
		Bodorgan No. 2 Tunnel 115yds. (105m)
72	Bodorgan	
75	Ty Croes	
81	Valley	Stanley Embankment ¾ mile (1.2km)
		Widening of Telford's Holyhead road embankment.
84¼	HOLYHEAD	

Initially apart from Chester and Holyhead fourteen intermediate stations designed by Francis Thompson were allocated for the line those as mentioned in the major construction list, and it was only after a presentation of a petition in 1846 that the station at Valley was added.

The station at Chester was contracted as a joint property between the Holyhead and Chester Railway, the Grand Junction Railway, the Chester and Birkenhead Railway (renamed the Birkenhead, Lancashire, and Cheshire Railway) and the Shropshire Union Railway. Contracted by Thomas Brassey who was born in Buerton Cheshire on 7th November 1805. The foundation stone was laid down in August 1847 and the station was opened on the 1st August 1848.

At Holyhead in July 1848 station facilities for passengers travelling by railway were very minimal, with only a temporary wooden station available which was built within six weeks at a cost of £800. This was situated one mile (1.6km) from the Admiralty Pier where the packet boats were berthed, and passengers were transferred by horse drawn omnibuses to and from the station to the pier. In 1851 a permanent town station was built on a site opposite to the present Holborn Rd. which opened on the 14th September. An extension line to the Admiralty Pier was also constructed which allowed initially the passage of horse drawn railway carriages, this line opened on the 20th May 1851. The extension works involved a cutting 587yds. (534m) in length, and a line on which the carriages were to be drawn, and the building of a 880yds. (801m) timber viaduct alongside the harbour cliffs and a timber drawbridge to the pier, and in all ten properties had to be demolished to allow access. However the new line had its draw backs in that the curves were so acute which necessitated four horses to draw the diminutive railway carriages, eventually the curves were eased and a rail siding was built and the horses were replaced by steam engines. The estimated cost of the various developments were £6,852 for the building land and the purchase of the Royal Hotel (formerly the Eagle and Child), £19,793 for the line to the pier, and £2,800 for the station which was designed by Charles Reed.

Further developments of the pier line took place to accommodate larger and heavier trains, although the line was not suitable for the heavy engines of the main line, therefore trains had to be worked to and from Holyhead Station and the Admiralty Pier by small 0-6-0 saddle tank engines.

Author's collection

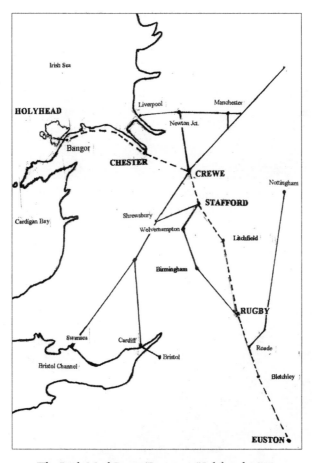

The Irish Mail Route Euston to Holyhead 1848
Euston to Rugby former London & Birmingham Rly.
Rugby to Stafford former Trent Valley Rly.
Stafford to Crewe former Grand Junction Rly.
Crewe to Chester former Chester & Crewe Rly.
Chester to Holyhead former Chester & Holyhead Rly.

Author's collection

Print of the 'Royal Hotel', purchased by the L.N.W. Rly. 1851
Formerly the 'Eagle and Child', 18th Century Coaching Inn
D. Lloyd Hughes & D. M. Williams
'The Story of Port' 1981
Courtesy Mrs Sian Murphy

Chester and Holyhead Railway
View at Penmaenmawr of the rail viaduct built 1848, and the upper
road viaduct which was built at a later date
Author's collection

The Chester to Holyhead line opened as far as Bangor on the1st May 1848 and the section from Llanfair P.G. to Holyhead on the1st August 1848. It was not until the Britannia Bridge was completed and opened on 5th March 1850 that the through line was fully opened. In the meantime passengers were carried by coaches between Bangor and Llanfair P.G.

The total cost of the whole construction of the line was £2,350,000.

Chester and Holyhead Railway
View of the avalanche shelter built over the railway at
Penmaenmawr 1848

Author's collection

Chester and Holyhead Railway
View of the 'Malltraeth' 19 arch viaduct on Anglesey 1848

Author's collection

Chapter 4

Three Bridges

The Dee Bridge

Designed By Robert Stephenson

The Dee bridge although the early intention was to build a five arch brick bridge adjoining the forty five brick arch viaduct approach to the River Dee, but due to foundation problems a plan for a cast iron bridge was substituted. The construction of this bridge incorporated laying three cast iron spans of 98ft. for each track, which rested on stone abutments and two stone piers, these were supported by two composite girders of 107ft. 6inch. in three sections. Connecting the composite girders were tensioned wrought iron tie bars. At the end of each girder was a quadrant shaped casting which was bolted to the stonework of the abutment and piers, further linked by wrought iron tension bars. The distance of 12ft. between the girders were spanned by 8x10inch. and 10x10inch. oak joists. Above these planking was laid lengthwise to provide a base for the iron chairs and rails.

One line of the bridge was opened in September 1846 for the sole use of the contractors, following a weight test of three engines and tenders totalling 90 tons which passed over without any incident. By November 1846 the bridge was in regular use by trains of the Shrewsbury and Chester Railway.

On the 24th May 1847 one of the southern girders on the western span fractured and fell as the 6/15pm S&C train from Chester was passing over. The train consisting of the engine, tender, four passenger carriages and a luggage van was travelling at an estimated 30mph (48km/h). Although the engine succeeded in crossing the bridge pulling its tender which had derailed, the carriages separated from the train and fell 36ft. into the river below, resulting in the deaths of the fireman who had fallen off the tender and a further five passengers. A further eight were injured.

At the following inquest in June 1847 reference was made to vibration and girder deflection of the bridge when trains passed over, inferring that the bridge was unsafe. However it was reported that similar bridges built before and after the Dee bridge were structurally sound. The inquest heard that the train had proceeded safely over the first and second spans of the bridge, but when it reached the middle of the third span approximately 50ft. from the abutment the driver felt the engine sinking under him, he thereby he increased speed in an attempt to clear the bridge before any disaster occurred, unfortunately the derailed tender struck the lateral ties causing further damage to the structure. Also reported was that a previous derailment of a train on the bridge had caused undue strain on the girders. However this evidence was not substantiated. It was deduced that the fracture of the girder took place at the middle and not at the abutment end. Railway commissioners James Walker and Capt. Simmons were critical in their submissions, in that calculations made by Stephenson of a safe load of 180tons was in fact only 106tons and that the weight of 18tons of stone recently laid as ballast for protecting the woodwork against hot cinders had further reduced the breaking weight of the girder. It was also reported that the tension bars had stretched and basically at the time of the accident the girders were taking the full weight.

In the findings, it was established that the girder had fractured because of insufficient strength to bear the pressure of quick trains over it. This resulted in all cast iron bridges throughout the railway system being examined and strengthened or reconstructed.

The Dee bridge was repaired and supported by timber piles, and a single line of track was opened on 20th July 1847. After a further inspection by Capt. Simmons the bridge was fully reopened on 23rd April 1848, with a recommendation for low speeds when crossing. By 1891 all cast iron underlying bridges were replaced, with The Dee bridge being rebuilt in brick and wrought iron in 1870–71.

With regards to Robert Stephenson, although this incident had left his reputation somewhat bruised and was probably the lowest point of his career he survived the Dee Bridge disaster, not only because he was held in high esteem, but also because it was only a question of time with the then knowledge available before a similar accident could have happened to other engineers. He was given the full backing of the Chester and Holyhead Railway directors, and his reputation was fully restored with his magnificent building of the Conway and Britannia bridges

The Conway Bridge
Designed by Robert Stephenson

The main contractor was Mr William Evans

The foundation stone of the bridge was laid on 12th May 1846 by the resident engineer Mr A. A. Ross.

The bridge construction consisted of two wrought iron box girder tubular sections carrying both the up and down lines across the River Conway which were fitted into piers in the abutments on both banks of the river.

The architecture for the two towers and abutments were built in effect to coincide with the structure of the castle and were designed by Francis Thompson. Built with Penmon and Great Orme limestone and Runcorn sandstone in courses varying from 15inch. to 3ft. thickness. To accommodate the positioning and the raising of the tubes, recesses were constructed in the stonework which were subsequently filled in when the tubes were at their planned height.

The tubes were constructed of wrought iron plates varying from ¼inch. to 1inch. in thickness riveted together and strengthened by T irons. To give additional strength cells were formed both at the top and bottom of the tube. The upper cells were 1ft. 9inch. high by 1ft. 8¼inch. wide, of which there were eight in number. The lower cells six in number were 2ft. 3½inch. wide by1ft. 9inch. high. The tubes were 14ft. wide by 22ft. 3½inch. high at the ends and 25ft. 6inch. at the centre and the total length being 412ft. (125m). The approximate weight of each tube was 1300tons.

The construction of the tubes began on 14th March 1847 and was carried out on the shoreline 100yds. (91m) from the piers, built on platforms 420ft. in length by 40ft. wide supported at 12ft. centres on frames carried on short piles. Two cranes were used in the building and one for unloading the metal plates brought in by ship. Workshops were erected alongside the platforms housing a steam engine for the drilling, shearing, and punching machines, needed to work the metal plates, also accommodated were furnaces for producing the hot rivets. The punching machine required a force of 46tons to pierce a 1inch. hole in ¾ inch. plate. At first 2800 holes could be punched in a day, but with advances in machinery 3000 holes per hour was achieved. The riveting gangs consisted of two riveters, a holder up, and two boys equipped with pinchers for delivering the hot rivets. The tubes once completed were then floated out across the river to their planned positions between the abutments.

By January 1848 the first tube for the up line was ready for moving, prior to this two temporary piers had been built at each end of the tube for support. This allowed the platform on which it had been built to be removed and the underneath to be excavated to allow six pontoons to be erected, three at each end. The pontoons were 95ft. long, 25ft. wide, and 8ft. deep, each capable of supporting a load of 460tons, also they were fitted with pumps and valves to allow them to be flooded and emptied as required.

Floating of the first tube began at high tide on 6th March 1848. In charge of the was Capt. Claxton RN. along with experienced seamen from Liverpool who with their nautical knowledge controlled the ropes and capstans required in the moving. However all did not go well at first due to one of the pontoons snagging a rock at the Conway side. It was 11th March before the tube was in its final position ready for lifting. At each end of the tube a lifting beam was fixed transversally to which hydraulic presses that were positioned in the abutments were attached by means of chains. Each chain link was 6ft. in length. The tube was raised 6ft. one link length a time until it reached a position 3ft. above its final level, here an extra 6ft. of prefabricated tube was added to each end of the tube to provide adequate bearing on the bed plates and expansion rollers in the abutments, and when the underfilling of the recesses by stonework was completed the tube was laid on to its final and permanent bed on 16th April, 18 ft. above high water. The tube was permanently fixed on the Conway side whilst the other end rested on eleven rollers and bed plates to allow for atmospheric changes in temperature. The track for the permanent way was laid down within two days. After final inspection the first locomotive passed over the bridge on the 18th April 1848 with Robert Stephenson on the footplate and the bridge was approved for single line traffic on 1st. May.

The floating of the second tube for the down line began on 12th October 1848. However a cause for concern arose in the lifting when one of the crossheads on the hydraulic presses cracked and immediate underbuilding of the recesses took place to support the tube. Fortunately the damaged crosshead managed to survive the final 2ft. 3inch. of lift and the tube was finally bedded down on the 8th December. The Bridge passed its final survey on the 2nd January 1849 thereby allowing it to be fully opened for traffic.

The incident of the damaged press led to a complete redesign of the lifting gear for the Britannia Bridge.

Robert Stephensons' 'Conway Tubular Bridge' built 1849
Photo of the 'Down rail Tube'. Showing new supports cylinders
incorporated in 1899. Required to add bearing to the span due to
the increasing weight capacity of trains.
Author's collection

In 1899 it became apparent that due to increasing weight capacity of trains the deflection of the bridge was gradually increasing.

'Deflection.' 'The amount a structure curves down when under weight and pressure at the centre.'

This was rectified by introducing underneath new cast iron support cylinders which reduced the bearing of the span from 400ft. (121mtrs.) to 310ft. (94mtrs.) The construction of which was carried out by The Cleveland Bridge and Engineering Co.

The Britannia Bridge
Designed by Robert Stephenson

Edwin Clarke was resident engineer with engineers William Fairburn and Eaton Hodgkinson acting as consultants. A workforce of about 1500 men were employed in its construction.

Work began on 10th April 1846 with the preparations of the foundations which were of solid rock. At the centre of the Menai Straits was a rock outcrop called the Britannia Rock (hence the Britannia Bridge) and on this the central tower was positioned. The bridge consisted of the central tower (The Britannia) two side towers which were constructed on land, two abutments and two portals, these supported eight box girder tubes; four to each line. The height of the towers were set to give a clearance of at least 100ft. (30.3mtrs.) in accordance with Admiralty requirements.

The height of the Towers
> The Britannia 221ft. 3inch. (67.2mtrs.)
> Side Towers 203ft. (62mtrs.)

The height of the Abutments

> The Arfon side 88ft. (27mtrs.)
>
> The Anglesey side 143ft. (44mtrs.)

Constructed of Penmon limestone, Runcorn Sandstone, and internal brickwork. The base of the Britannia Tower is 60ft. by 50ft. 5inch. wide with walls 8ft. to 10ft. thick which tapered 1in 36 on all sides. Built into the Britannia Tower were two recesses on each side and on the land towers two recesses on the waterside only, these were required when positioning the tubes ready for raising.

The box girder tubes were in two sizes, the four centre or water tubes were 460ft. (140mtrs.) and the four land tubes 230ft. (70mtrs.) in length. The four shorter land tubes were built in situ to the land towers supported during construction by timber platforms and surrounded by wooden scaffolding. The four centre tubes were constructed on shore on the Caernarvonshire side on specially prepared timber platforms similar to those at Conway by Messrs. Nowell, Hemingway and Pearson, who were contractors for all masonry and scaffolding.

To accommodate the workforce eighty cottages were built, along with shops, a school, Sunday school, and a meeting place, these were situated on the banks of the Straits adjacent to the bridge. To aid construction there were three steam engines and twenty six travelling cranes which were used to raise building materials to the towers, and unload shipping that brought in metal plates, building material, and stores, in all 2177 loads were brought in by ship.

Construction of the four water tubes to the same design as those at Conway began on 10th August 1847 when the first rivet was inserted by Edwin Clarke, they were constructed by Messrs. Garforth of Dukinfield,and Mr C.C. Mare of Blackwall London. On completion of the tubular sections the timber platforms were systematically removed in order that the pontoons could be positioned underneath and were then floated out independently to the awaiting towers and their required positions. Situated in the recesses they were then raised into place by hydraulic press raising machinery positioned in the towers, which were made by the bank Quay Foundry in Warrington As each tube was slowly raised the recesses were under filled with brickwork and timber to avoid any accidents.

The raising of the first tube began on the 10th August 1849 between the centre tower and the Anglesey side tower and the joining of this tube and the land tube was completed by 10th November 1849. It was however not with out incident, when only 24ft. (7.2mtrs.) up the lifting machinery in the Anglesey tower failed which resulted in the tube dropping 9inch. on to the brickwork and packing below it. Unfortunately one workman was killed and several others had narrow escapes from being crushed. Again on completion of the lifting when the machinery was being removed from the Anglesey tower to the Caernarvon tower for the second lift a section of the machinery fell on to the masonry below causing a second fatality and the injury of several workmen.

To prioritise, work was concentrated on the Up line and the second centre tube was raised into place by 7th January 1850. Over the next two months work was carried out riveting the four tubes together and laying the track. The completed tube was fixed in the Britannia tower and expansion and contraction given to atmospheric conditions was overcome by means of rollers in the other towers and abutments.

With the completion of the Up line across the bridge, on the 5th March 1850 three trains were assembled at Bangor station in readiness for the first crossing headed by three

'Crewe Type' engines, No. 31 2-2-2 Pegasus, No. 205 2-4-0 St. David, and No. 249 2-4-0 Cambrian. At 6/30am the first train left Bangor on board were Mr Robert Stephenson, Mr Trevithick, Locomotive Manager of the L.N.W.R. and Messrs. Bidder, Clark, and Appold. The train arrived at the bridge at 7am and proceeded to make the first crossing at a steady 7m.p.h. (11kmph) to prove the soundness of the structure. This was followed by a second train of 21 heavily laden wagons of Brymbo coal with a weight including the engine of 300 tons and travelling at between 8 to 10m.p.h. on board were Mr F. Foster engineer, Mr Lee resident engineer, Mr J. C. Mare constructor of the tubes, Mr Burger manager of the line and Messrs Hedworth, Rolfe, MacLaren, Borthwick, and Gooch. After traversing the bridge as an act of completion the final 2,000,000th. rivet was put in to the structure by Mr Mare, and driven home by Mr Robert Stephenson. A further test of the bridge was then carried out which required the coal wagons of 200 tons being positioned at the centre of the Caernarvon side tube for two hours. This was successful as there was no adverse effect to the structure. At 12 noon the last test took place when a train of three engines, the coal wagons, and between 30 to 40 railway carriages carrying 600 to 700 people crossed the bridge to Llanfair P.G. then across Anglesey finally arriving in Holyhead where a tremendous reception awaited.

On the 15th March Capt. Simmons the Board of Trade inspector made a survey of the whole structure of the bridge and found only a slight deflection in the tubes with a load of 250 tons and placed every confidence in its construction.

Located on either side of the track at the two entrances to the bridge as though guarding both approaches were placed four huge carved limestone figures of lions on pedestals. The work of John Thomas, born at Chelford in

Gloucestershire of Welsh ancestry. Each figure was constructed in eleven sections with a weight of 30 tons and measured 35ft. (10.6mtrs.) in length and 12ft. (3.6mtrs.) high.

The first London passenger train left Holyhead at 2/30pm on 18th March 1850 arriving at London Euston at 11pm.

In April 1850 work proceeded on the down line of tubes and the last lift was completed by August. The two lines of tubes were then braced together to counteract any possible oscillation due to high winds. Also constructed in the tubes were loopholes at regular intervals to offer ventilation, light, and above all the removal of steam and smoke from passing engines. A final Board of Trade inspection was carried out on the 19th October when permission was given for the opening to through traffic.

Floating of the second 'Water' tube of the Britannia Bridge
Lithograph by George Hawkins 1849
D. Lloyd Hughes & D. M. Williams
'The Story of Port' 1981
Courtesy Mrs Sian Murphy

The total length of the bridge was 1511ft. (459mtrs.), each line of tubes weighed 5,188 tons. The full weight of the whole construction resting on the foundations was 29,000 tons. The total cost of the building was £674,000.

The Britannia Bridge survived without damage until 13th June 1946 when during repainting the carelessness of a painter using a blow-lamp set fire to some of the rail sleepers causing the track to buckle. This resulted in the bridge being closed to all traffic for six hours, until single line working could be reinstalled on the Up line. The Down line remained closed for four days. 24 years later, on the 23rd May 1970 the bridge was irreparably damaged by boys who accidentally set fire to the bridge inside the tubular structure whilst mischievously looking for birds nests. The lit paper torch they were carrying dropped into the well between the rails igniting the miscellaneous litter that had accumulated there which in turn set fire to the sleepers and tarred roof. Unfortunately the meticulous clearing of litter from the

Egyptian stone lions sculpted by John Thomas guarding the approach to the abutments of the Britannia Bridge, taken from the Caernarvon side. Distant light can be seen at the end of the down line tube.

H. D. Bowtell
Courtesy The Manchester Locomotive Society
Archives

track had deteriorated somewhat with the demise of the steam engine. With a wind blowing from the South West fire raged throughout the tubes causing the ironwork to sag rendering it unsafe for further use. The bridge was redesigned by Husband & Co. as consultants to British Rail and was rebuilt by the Cleveland Bridge and engineering Co. and it reopened in 1972. The towers and abutments remained, however the tubes were removed and replaced by a two deck bridge supported by steel archways. The lower deck carries the rail track whilst the one above carries the carriageway of the A55 trunk road.

The construction of the Britannia Bridge unfortunately did not come without casualties. In St. Mary's churchyard at Llanfair P.G. there is a memorial tombstone in the shape of an obelisk erected to the memory of the men who died of injuries received during the construction of the bridge.

Print from a painting by T. Picken 1862,
depicting Telford's Menai Suspension Bridge and Stevenson's
Britannia Bridge
Courtesy The National Library of Wales

Conference of the Britannia Bridge engineers
(centre Robert Stephenson)

Courtesy The Institution of Civil Engineers & Bridge Books

The monument erected in St Mary's churchyard Llanfair P.G. Anglesey. In memory of those who lost their lives during the construction of the Britannia Bridge.

Named as follows on the memorial are:

George Moore	December 1846	John Williams	June 1849
Robert Parry	November 1847	Owen Parry	August 1849
Samuel Davies	December 1847	John Thompson	November 1849
William Blayloc	December 1847	John Williams	November 1849
Richard Edwards	February 1848	William Lewis	March 1850
William Howard (Boy)	March 1848	David Lewis	October 1850
George Hughes	March 1848	Isaac Garforth	March 1850
William Jones	? 1848		of Muirfield, Yorkshire
Henry Jones	July 1848		bricklayer, aged 62 yrs.

Also commemorated is William Brook of Dewsbury, Yorkshire. Principal accountant to Messrs Nowell, Hemingway and Pearson contractors for the masonry, who died 11th October 1847 aged 27 yrs. of Typhus Fever.

A further sad inclusion is that of Emma Greaves daughter of James Greaves of Lake Lock, Wakefield, Yorkshire. Who died at the Britannia Bridge on December 1849 aged 5 yrs.

During the reconstruction of the bridge a further two fatalities occurred and are commemorated.

Graham Parry	February 1972
William Owen	February 1973

Author's collection

Chapter 5

Transference of Mails from Coach to Train

The 1830's saw the peak of the postal mail coach service within Gt. Britain, with mail coaches running from London to all the main towns. These were operated by contractors under defined agreements with the Post Office. In 1837 twenty eight mail coaches left London daily, three of which went to Scotland and two to Wales, of these three had connections to Ireland. However further improvements in this mode of transport was limited, based mainly on the ultimate speed and physical endurance of the horses involved. The average speed with which the coaches ran was 10mph (16km). The Post Office was handling 82 million letters a year which were charged at varying costs to the public based on distance. e.g. London to Liverpool 11d. and to Aberdeen 1s. 3d. The main priority was the speed of delivery, therefore a means to further reduce travelling times and to standardise costs needed to be addressed.

In 1827 the London financier Thomas Richardson had the vision to write to the secretary of the post office Francis Freeling to try and interest him as to the possibility of conveying mails by the newly emerging railways. However it was not until the Liverpool and Manchester Rly. came into being that Freeling saw the potential of this new development in transport. Presentations were made by Freeling to the two postmasters in Liverpool and Manchester outlining his suggestions of mail being transported by rail, and in doing so requested their observations on the matter. Both reacted favourably, and with their joint agreement meetings were arranged with the L. & M. Rly. Co. After some earnest bargaining a contract was formalised for the conveyance of mails between the two cities. So began the transference of mails to the railways.

Throughout the 1840's and 50's the nationwide emergence of numerous railway companies that linked all large towns and cities provided for the Post Office a speedier delivery service, and also the ability to carry larger quantities of mail.

The capability of the earliest trains to reach average speeds of 20 (32km) to 30mph (48km) thereby more than halfing the transit time eventually brought about the ultimate decline in horse drawn mail coaches. Further technical developments in the railways realised the production of larger and faster engines, and by 1860 the contract with the Post Office required that trains ran at an average speed of 42mph (67km).

When the Bills for the London & Birmingham and Grand Junction Railway was placed before parliament in 1833 a clause was entered for free conveyance of mail, but there was strong opposition from the two prospective railway companies. As a result the Post Office had to make reciprocal arrangements with each of the them and also with other emerging railways. The need for a formal statuary basis for the conveyance of mails to be carried by railways came into exsistence by an Act of 1838. In this it required the railway companies to carry mails on twenty eight days notice at times fixed by the post Office, on terms reached by mutual agreement or arbitration. In economic terms, in 1838 the Post Office paid the railways £1313 for the mail contract, by 1852 this had risen considerably to £194,000.

Further developments for improving the speed of mail delivery was the introduction of the travelling post office on 6th January 1838 where mail was sorted on route. Also an apparatus for dispatching and collecting of mails whilst the train was at speed without stopping at minor stations further reduced travelling times.

To reduce the cost of postage, Rowland Hill of the Post Office in 1840 introduced the penny post, after observing that the high cost of postage had diminished the postal revenue over a period of time. Whereas in France due to low postage rates the revenue had increased substantially.

The mails to Ireland were first carried by rail on the 24th January 1839 via Birmingham on the London & Birmingham Rly. then by the Grand Junction Rly. via Crewe to Newton Junction, and then by the Liverpool & Manchester Rly. to Liverpool. The mails were then shipped to Kingstown by Admiralty packet boats which had been transferred from the Holyhead route. The average time taken to carry the mails from London To Dublin was about 25 hours. The mail left London at 8pm, arriving in Liverpool for the 9am sailing to Kingstown which took about 12hrs. In addition to the Admiralty packets the Post office in 1844 also contracted with the City of Dublin Steam Packet Co. for the conveying of mails from Liverpool.

*** Post Office Mail Deliveries UK 1839–1900 in millions

	Letters	Postcards	Newspapers & Packets	Parcels
1839	82	-	-	-
1840	169	-	-	-
1850	346	-	-	-
1856	478	-	74	-
1860	564	-	82	-
1872	885	76	223	-
1880	1128	115	345	-
1885	1360	160	464	22
1890	1650	217	602	43
1900	2247	401	866	75

*** (Second Abstract of British Historical Statistics: B. R. Mitchell & H. G. Jones)

Chapter 6

Formation of the
London and North Western Railway
(L.N.W.R.) (i)
The Trent Valley Line (ii)
Standard Time (iii)

The L.N.W.R. was created in 1846 by the two largest railway companies, The London and Birmingham Railway and The Grand Junction Railway along with the Manchester and Birmingham Railway.

Prior to the formation, relations between the L.B.R. and the G.J.R. were amicable, with both railways running into and out of Birmingham. Unfortunately with both companies seeking expansion disagreement and differences developed between them to the extent of outright hostility.

The G.J.R. merged with the Liverpool and Manchester Rly. and was looking further to join the North Union Rly. under construction to Preston. Whereas the L & B joined with the Manchester & Birmingham Rly. which was seeking a separate line south to London which would bypass Crewe. This move prompted the G.J.R. to rethink its seeking of a southern route to London and contemplated to change to broad gauge line to link up with the Great Western Railway with a possible route to Paddington in London. Although never a feasable conception it prompted the L & B to renew its relations with the G.J.R. which finally brought about the amalgamation of the two companies.

The Act to create the new L.N.W.R. received Royal Assent on 16th July 1846. In total it had 405 miles (648km) of track and incorporated 114 stations The total capital was £17,242,310, with further investments this brought the sum to £21,929,810, making it the largest stock company in the 19th century.

Eventually the L.N.W.R. reached Scotland through the cooperation with the Caledonian Railway, thereby linking most of Britain's, largest cities.

The Trent Valley line
Initially the Trent Valley Line was owned by an independent company who started construction on the line in 1845. However whilst it was still being built it was taken over by the L.N.W.R. It was 50 miles (66km) in length and ran from Rugby to Stafford, the purpose of which was to give a more direct route to the North West bypassing Birmingham.

The contractor was Thomas Brassey in partnership with Robert Stephenson and William MacKenzie. The engineers were Robert Stephenson, George Bidder, and Thomas Gooch.

Thirteen stations were built on the route along with the engineering of fourteen major bridges and also one tunnel. This tunnel at Shugborough being the largest of the engineering work. It was 777yds. (708mtrs.) long and built on a curve and brick lined throughout. It passed under the Satnall Hills in the grounds of Shugborough Hall.

Stations

RUGBY	Atherstone	Rugeley
Brinklow	Polesworth	Colwich
Shilton	TAMWORTH	Milford & Brocton
Bulkington	LICHFIELD	STAFFORD
NUNEATON		

The line officially opened on 30th November 1847.

Standard Time

In the 1780's it was accepted that time differed as one moved East or West of Greenwich. During that period the differences in local times was irrelevant as nobody moved fast enough for it to cause any serious problem. For example the difference in time between East Anglia and Cornwall was half an hour. There were variations in local times along the route but it was insignificant as it caused little disruption.

With the evolving railway system a reason to change became apparent as time tables required time to be precise However not all railway companies adhered to this due to local prejudices. Henry Booth the secretary of the Liverpool & Manchester Rly. was in favour of a standard time in 1845 and petitioned Parliament for its adoption. The Railway Clearing House passed a resolution recommending the adoption of Greenwich time and most companies complied to its introduction, but in some areas hostility by some whose insistance of change of local time was seen as railway agression. For instance when the Chester and Holyhead Railway came into being they regulated all their clocks along the route by the Craig-y-Don gun, 16½ minutes after Greenwich which caused something of a dilemma, as the Irish mail took its time from Greenwich.

In the West Country hostility arose as traditionalists were determined to retain their local independence. It was brought to a conclusion when the Dean of Exeter directed that the cathedral clock be advanced 14 minutes on the 2 November 1852 the day after the first time signal had begun to arrive by the newly completed telegraph system lying adjacent to the railway thereby complying to Greenwich time. This occurrence resulted in the establishment of a commonplace time system for the whole country. It was not until 1880 that the Statute (Definition of Time Act) laid down that Greenwich time was to be universal for the whole of Gt. Britain.

Chapter 7

The First Irish Mail Train
and the Mail up to 1860

There is some confusion as to the inaugural date of the first
Irish Mail, some sources date this as Tuesday 1st. August
1848, whereas respectfully Peter E. Baughan in his book
'The Chester and Holyhead Railway' queries this, and
indicates probably it was the previous day, and that being,
the Irish Mail departed London Euston at 8/45pm on the
31st July 1848. This is substantiated by a report in the *North
Wales Chronicle* newspaper dated 8th August 1848 that the
mail train arrived in Holyhead at 9am on the 1st. August.
Therefore it is assumed that the first 'Down' Irish Mail left
Euston at 8/45pm on the 31st July 1848 carrying both mails
and first and second class passengers.

The train was under the auspices of the L.N.W.R. from
London to Chester, where from there to Holyhead it was
the responsibility of the Chester and Holyhead Rly. Co.

**Extract from the *North Wales Chronicle* Tuesday 8th
August 1848.**
'On Tuesday 1st inst., the line of Railway was opened
through Anglesey in continuation of the part previously
opened to Bangor. H.M. Packet Banshee and the Chester
and Holyhead Rly. Co's Cambria arrived from Liverpool in
the afternoon of Monday to take their place on station the
following day.

The mail train due at 6/45am did not arrive until 9am.
Having taken the mail and passengers on board the Banshee
immediately sailed for Kingstown. At 3pm the Caradoc

arrived from Kingstown with the mail and 75 passengers.

The pierhead was thronged with omnibuses, stage coaches and cars to convey passengers and their luggage to the Railway Station. And such a number of spectators was not seen on the pierhead since the landing of George 1V in August 1821. Most of the shops were closed, and the day was observed as a Holiday by the inhabitants in commemoration of the event. Immediately after the arrival of the packet an express train left, and the Mail at 6/20pm both containing several carriages filled with passengers. The commencement bespoke favourably for the company.

After the arrival of the express train, the Company's boat *Cambria* sailed at 7pm for Kingstown.'

Time Table 1848

'Down Irish Mail'

Dep.	London	8.45pm		Dep.	Crewe	2.35am
~	Watford	9.15pm		~	Beeston	3.16am
~	Tring	9.53pm		~	Chester	3.45am
					(New Station)	
					1/8/48	
~	Wolverton	10.40pm		~	Flint	4.03am
~	Roade	11.10pm		~	Holywell	4.13am
~	Blisworth	11.27pm		~	Rhyl	4.36am
~	Rugby	11.58pm	Trent ~		Conway	5.05am
~	Nuneaton	12.30am	–	Arr.	Bangor	5.25am
~	Tamworth	12.58am	Valley	Dep.	Llanfair P.G.	
						6am *
~	Lichfield	1.10am	–	Arr.	Holyhead	
						6.45am *
~	Stafford	1.40am	Line			
~	Whitmore	2.10am		Arr.	Kingstown	
					approx. 5hrs later	

* The Mail train terminated at Bangor due to the Britannia bridge being under construction and passengers and mails

were transferred by coaches via Telford's suspension bridge to Llanfair P.G. to complete the journey by rail across Anglesey to Holyhead and was due to arrive as is shown at 6/45am. The report in the *North Wales Chronicle* states the arrival as 9am. The Anglesey part of the line also opened on the 1st August 1848. The next train to arrive was the 9am express out of Euston which was tabled to arrive at 5/45pm after embarking passengers, the C&H Rly. steamer *Cambria* sailed for Kingstown at 7pm.

* Arrival timings are somewhat debatable with the ongoing transference of passengers from Bangor to Llanfair P.G.

The first 'Up' mail to London on the 1st August after the arrival of the Admiralty packet 'Caradoc' departed Holyhead at 6/20pm.

Coach transfer at Llanfair

Dep., Bangor 7/50pm

Dep. Chester 9/25pm

*Arr. Euston 4/45am

In order for the section of the line across Anglesey to become operational two engines were shipped from Liverpool to Holyhead. These probably were the 'Tayleur' 4-2-0 Long Boiler engines that although ordered by the C&H Rly. they were listed in the locomotive stock of the L.N.W.R. (See Chapter 9)

There is one fact of interest prior to the 'Down' mail leaving Euston, an Admiralty messenger from Greenwich handed over to the guard of the Irish Mail a chronometer (watch) in a leather case which had been set at Greenwich time. On arrival at Holyhead it was handed over to the Master of the mail boat sailing for Kingstown, whilst also all station clocks at Holyhead were synchronized to that time. At Kingstown it was passed to the Harbour Master who dispatched it to the Ballast Office at Dublin Port. Where being the official Greenwich time it was signified by the dropping of a metal ball situated on top of the building at exactly midday. Due to the longitudinal difference between Greenwich and Dublin there was a 25 minute variance between that and local time. The watch was then returned via the 'Up' mail to the Admiralty in London for any readjustment. Even with the introduction of the telegraph and telephone this procedure continued every day until 1949. It came to be known as the 'King's Time'.

This time table and procedure continued until 1850. When following the opening to traffic on 15th March 1850 of a single line working of the 'Up' line across the Britannia Bridge realised a through rail connection between London Euston and Holyhead. The bridge became fully operational when the 'Down' line was completed and opened after a Board of Trade inspection on the 19th October 1850. The opening of the Bridge resulted in a second express train being introduced which left London at 5pm, with the original 'Irish Mail' remaining at its 8/45pm departure time. However the route taken by the two trains differed in that the 5pm train was routed via Birmingham whereas the 8/45pm train was routed by the Trent Valley Line.

Time Table 1850 as follows:

5pm (Down) Express

Dep.	London	5pm	Dep.	Chester	10.23pm
~	Wolverton	6.15pm	~	Holywell	10.50pm
~	Rugby	7.05pm	~	Rhyl	11.12pm
~	Coventry	7.25pm	~	Conway	11.45pm
Arr.	Birmingham	8pm	~	Bangor	12.10am
Dep.	Birmingham	8.15pm	Arr.	Holyhead	1.05am
~	Wolverhampton	8.37pm			
~	Stafford	9.02pm	Arr.	Kingstown	6.15am
				* approx.	
~	Crewe	9.42pm			

8.45pm (Down) Irish Mail

Dep.	London	8.45pm	Dep.	Chester	3.06am
~	Watford	9.15pm	~	Flint	3.34am
~	Tring	9.45pm	~	Holywell	3.44am
~	Bletchley	10.11pm	~	Rhyl	4.09am
~	Wolverton	10.24pm	~	Conway	4.39am
~	Blisworth	10.47pm	~	Bangor	5.04am
~	Weedon	11.04pm	~	Llanfair	5.19am
~	Rugby	11.31pm	Arr.	Holyhead	5.49am
~	Nuneaton	11.59pm			
~	Tamworth	12.25am	Arr.	Kingstown	11am
				* approx.	
~	Lichfield	12.40am			
~	Stafford	1.12am			
~	Crewe	2.03am			

'Up' Mail			'Up' Mail		
Dep.	Kingstown	1.pm	Dep.	Kingstown	7.30pm
~	Holyhead	7pm	~	Holyhead	2am
Arr.	London	4.50am	Arr.	London	11am

Under an act of the 23rd July 1855 for 'The Improved Postal and Passenger Communication with Ireland', the C.H.Rly. accepted on the 1st July 1856 terms that the L.N.W.R. should work the C.H.Rly. as an integral part of its own system. It was not however until 1st. January 1859 that full amalgamation came into force.

In 1860 a new postal agreement for the transportation of the Royal Mail was entered into by the Post Office, the L.N.W.R. and the C.D.S.P. Co. which resulted in a radical speedier and more efficient service of both mails and passengers.

Under the agreement the transit times of mail trains from London Euston to Holyhead was reduced to 6hrs. 40mins.

and the sea crossing to 4hrs. Allowing for the transference of mails and passengers an overall travelling time of 11hrs. was achieved, reducing the previous times by 3hrs. It was anticipated that the mail train would average a speed of 42 m.p.h. (67k.m.p.h.) something quite phenomenal for that period of time. This made the Irish Mail the fastest express in the country. A Travelling Post Office (TPO) with mail bag transfer apparatus was attached to the train where collection and distribution of mails on route added to the gain in transit time by removing the neccesity to stop at sixteen lesser privileged stations.

Changes in the time table in October1860 brought into effect a Day and Night service for the Irish Mail, leaving London Euston at 7.25am and 8.25pm respectively, stopping only at Rugby, Stafford and Chester on route. The Bradshaw time table for October 1860 states 'Passengers on these trains are booked to Ireland only'.

The time table required mail trains to run the 84 miles (134km) between Chester and Holyhead non stop in a little over 2hrs. In order to accomplish this water troughs 473yds. (430mtrs.) long, the first in the world and patented by John Ramsbottom the L.N.W.R. superintendent in 1860 were laid on both 'up' and 'down' tracks at Mochdre between Colwyn Bay and Conway which were fed by the Mochdre stream, this was under an agreement with Lord Mostyn. Engines mainly of the Problem or Lady Of the Lake class as they were known worked the Irish Mail at that time and they were fitted with water pick up scoops to enable them to pick up water at speed to replenish their stocks, whereas previously regular stops had to be made to refill with water. Eventually water troughs were laid down throughout the country where fast expresses were running. In 1871 due to scarcity of water supply at times by the Mochdre stream the troughs were removed from Mochdre and relayed one mile

Water troughs at Aber designed by John Robertson 1860.
The first in the world.
Laid at Mochdre in 1860 and relocated to Aber in 1871.
Photo of Stanier 'Black Five' picking up water on the up line.

Haram V. Stewart
'Centenary of The Irish Mail'

east of Aber where they were supplied by the River Aber. A forty year lease was agreed with Lord Penrhyn for the removal of water from the river, and this was constantly extended until it was cancelled in 1968 at the end of the steam era of engines.

The standard composition for the Irish Mail train for about this period was, brake van, two first and one second class carriages, travelling Post Office, mail van, parcel van, one first and three composite carriages (1st & 2nd), and a brake van. Twelve vehicles weighing about 240 tons. It must be realised that the size of the carriages were not as large of their later counterparts and as train loads increased it was not uncommon for the train to be 'double headed'. Gradually over the years as bigger and more powerful and high performance locomotives were introduced it was not unusual for the Irish Mail to be comprised of 15 plus large vehicles with a train weight in excess of 500 tons. This necessitated at times the requirement of a assistant 'banking engine' to negotiate the Camden bank out of Euston and the 1 in 90 gradient out of Holyhead.

Time table for the Irish Mail October 1860.

'Down Irish Mail'

Dep.	Euston	7.25am	Dep.	Euston	8.25pm
Arr.	Rugby	9.25am	Arr.	Rugby	10.25pm
Dep.	Rugby	9.28am	Dep.	Rugby	10.27pm
~	Stafford	10.40am **	~	Stafford	11.40pm **
Arr.	Chester	1.48am	Arr.	Chester	12.48am
Dep	Chester	11.58am	Dep.	Chester	12.58am
Arr.	Holyhead	2.05pm	Arr.	Holyhead	3.05am
~	Kingstown	6.05pm	~	Kingstown	7.05am

'Up Irish Mail'

Dep.	Kingston	7am	Dep.	Kingstown	7.30pm
~	Holyhead	11.40am	~	Holyhead	12.00am
Arr.	Chester	1.45pm	Arr.	Chester	2.05am
Dep.	Chester	1.55pm	Dep.	Chester	2.25am
~	Stafford	3.03pm **	~	Stafford	3.23am **
Arr.	Rugby	4.16pm	Arr.	Rugby	4.36am
Dep.	Rugby	4.19pm	Dep.	Rugby	4.39am
Arr.	Euston	6.25pm	Arr.	Euston	6.45am

** Change of engines
Euston to Stafford   L.N.W.R. Southern Division Engines
Stafford to Holyhead L.N.W.R. Northern Division Engines

*** Extracts from the diary of Thomas Baron, Fireman and Driver of the Irish Mail

Date	Engine No.	Driver Mileage	Fireman Remarks
Dec 2 1861	No. 561	T Jones 156	T Baron Stafford & Holyhead Irish Mail
Dec 7 1861	No. 561	T Jones 156	T Baron Stafford & Holyhead Mail
Dec 21 1861	No. 561	T Jones 156	T Baron Holyhead to Stafford & Crewe Mail
Dec 30 1861	No. 561	T Jones 156	T Baron Holyhead to Stafford & Crewe
Dec 31 1861	No. 561	T Jones 156	T Baron Crewe to Holyhead & Stafford

Engine No. 561 Problem Class Built 1861 and named Prince Oscar November 1862
*** Courtesy of Mr Edward Talbot

Chapter 8

The Mail Steamer Contract

The Chester and Holyhead Railway was built primarily to fulfill the task of conveying mail and passengers to Ireland. With little industrial development apart from quarrying in North Wales, and the area mostly of a rural nature and with the coastal towns yet to expand into holiday destinations that we know today, there was little in the way of commerce for the railway to exploit.

In 1847 the C&H Rly. placed a bill before Parliament for it to be allowed run its own steamers to Ireland from its terminus at Holyhead in anticipation of a cross channel mail contract with the Post Office. However opposition to this came from various shipping companies, the City of Dublin Steam packet Co. and the Steam Ship Owners Association to name just two, who were against the principal of a railway company being given powers to run ships which would take away trade from their companies.

At the time the board of the C&H Rly. request for steamer powers in order to run its own ships caused serious doubts amongst its shareholders as to its judgement, in view of the fact that the Admiralty had placed an order for four new packet boats. The *St. Columba* (694tons), *Banshee* (670tons), *Caradoc* (662tons) and the *Llewellyn* (654Tons), to run the mail contract when it was transferred back from Liverpool to Holyhead on completion of the railway. Undaunted the C&H proceeded to arrange contracts for four new vessels in 1848, two to be built in London the Anglia 473tons by Ditchburn and Mare, and the *Scotia* 479tons by Wigram & Company, one at Liverpool the *Hibernia* 573tons by Bury, Curtis and Kennedy, and the other the *Cambria* 590tons by Laird's of Birkenhead. All with a required speed of 14 knots.

The C&H Rly. presented a further Bill to Parliament in 1848 again for steamer services, and although opposition came from the House of Lords clauses were inserted in the bill that should the Admiralty cease to operate the mail service the C&H Rly. after notice would be given the authority. Royal Assent for the Bill was given on 22nd July 1848.

In June 1849 the Admiralty decided to withdraw its contract with City of Dublin Steam Packet Co. for the service between Liverpool and Kingstown and concentrate on its service with Admiralty packets from Holyhead.

*** The official return for December 1848 shows the average passage time for the Admiralty packet ships between Holyhead and Kingstown was as follows:

Banshee	4hr. 16min.
Llewellyn	4hr. 24min.
Caradoc	4hr. 34min.
St. Columba	5hr. 2min.

Due to distress in Ireland, and consequent drop in passenger numbers and with the Britannia Bridge link in the land mail service not yet completed the Admiralty were incurring losses on their cross channel service. The findings of a committee into the packet service revealed that mails were carried at less cost by hired packets than those of the Admiralty.

*** Sea Breezes 1961 Pg. 30

The proof of this was the service via Liverpool when the mail was carried by both Admiralty and the C of DSP Co.

The government therefore decided to withdraw the Admiralty packets from Holyhead and opted for private tender on the cross channel service. The C&H Rly. with its own ships anticipated that the contract with the Post Office would be offered to them and submitted two tenders, the lowest being £33,000 per annum over ten years plus the purchase of two of the Admiralty boats, a condition laid down by the Admiralty. However the C of DSP Co. who had worked the Liverpool service also submitted two tenders, the first being for £30,000 plus the purchase of two admiralty packet, and a second tender of £25,000 without the purchase of Admiralty boats. On March 8th 1850 the Post Office accepted the C of DSP Co. second tender much to the displeasure of the C&H Rly. The contract took effect on the 1st May 1850. The C of DSP Co. used an existing vessel the *Eblana* and purchased the *St. Columba* and *Llewellyn* from the Admiralty and hired the *Banshee* to inaugurate the service. The company then ordered a new vessel the *Prince Arthur* which came into service in 1851.

It is interesting to note that within the contract was a compensation clause in that the Post Office would implement a fine of £1-14s-0 (1.70p) for each minute late outside of the agreed scheduled transit time of the mail. It is speculation however that the fine was ever implemented, although it did have the effect that the 'Mail boat' sailed at all times irrespective of unfavourable weather conditions.

Although the mail contract came up for renewal at ten year intervals it remained with the C of DSP Co. for the next seventy years until in 1920 when finally the L.N.W.R. were successful in obtaining the contract, giving them overall control of the mail dispatch from London to Kingstown.

During the period up to 1920 the L.N.W.R. in its own right operated a Day and Night express passenger boat service to Dublin North Wall.

In 1860 on renewal of the contract with the Post Office and in order to succeed in reducing the sea journey between

Holyhead and Kingstown the C of DSP Co. replaced their existing ships with a quartette of new paddle steamers. Three of them, the *Ulster*, *Munster*, and *Connaught* were built by Lairds Bros. each having the particular feature of four funnels, whilst the fourth the Leinster was built by Samunda which had only two funnels. The funnels of the four ships were painted in the Cof DSP Co's distinctive black colour. The ships were 334ft. in length, with a beam of 35ft. each had a gross tonnage of 1421 tons and were capable of a speed of 17.5 knots Other features were deck cabins amidships, and sleeping cabins for both first and second class passengers in the forward part of the ship, also another important addition was the provision of an on board mail sorting office to speed up the delivery of mails.

In 1884 all four vessels underwent major refits, which included reboilering and the fitting of a longer poop deck which provided additional accommodation for both passengers and mails. Another alteration was that the three four funneled ships were reduced to only two funnels. The changes that were made increased the gross tonnage of the vessels to 1,713 tons.

To assist extra berthing of all vessels a jetty was added to the Admiralty Pier at Holyhead, whilst at Kingstown a new pier known as the Carlisle Pier was added this enabled trains to run alongside the Mail and Passenge ships berthed there, thereby offering a more convenient service.

'George IV' Arch on the Admiralty Pier built in 1821 to commemorate his visit to Holyhead whilst on his journey to Ireland. A 'City of Dublin' Royal Mail Steamer can be seen berthed alongside.

T. Selby collection

'City of Dublin' Royal Mail Paddle Steamer berthed at the Admiralty Pier circa 1895. One of four built in 1860, and named after the 'Four Irish Provinces' – Ulster, Munster, Leinster and Connaught, three of which had four funnels, the Leinster having just two. All were refitted in 1884, and carried only two funnels. They were taken out of service and sold in 1896 and 1897.

T. Selby collection

'City of Dublin' Royal Mail Steamer berthed at the Admiralty Pier
circa 1900. One of the four twin screwed ships built in 1895,
again named after the Four Provinces.
Two of which the Connaught, and Leinster were sunk in the
First World War.

T. Selby collection

Postcard circa 1900
Holyhead
Showing City of Dublin Mail Boats berthed at the Admiralty Pier.
G. S. Griffiths collection

Postcard of the City of Dublin Steam Packet co. circa 1895

Edward Watson
Royal Mail to Ireland 1917

Chapter 9

L.N.W.R. Locomotives of the 'Irish Mail'

The C&H Rly. first intended to operate its own locomotive power and had gone as far as to place an order with Chas. Tayleur & Co. in 1847 for six engines and were issued with works numbers 263 to 268 and to be named Britannia, Menai, Bangor, Caernarvon, Flint and Chester. The design was of a 'Stephenson' 4-2-0 Long Boiler type with round top fireboxes with raised casing and domes immediately behind the chimney, and with a wheel arrangement of two pairs of leading or 'bogey' wheels and a pair of 6ft. diameter driving wheels, coupled with a six wheeled tender with a tank capacity of 1000 gallons. However due to financial constraints the C&H Rly. were dependent on the L.N.W.R. for its provision of engines and rolling stock throughout its existence until it was amalgamated with the latter in 1865. It is questionable however that the C&H Rly. ever took delivery of these engines. Records show that the six engines ordered appeared on the list of the L.N.W.R. engines and were renumbered 176 to 181.

After the creation of the L.N.W.R. in 1846 three divisions were approved for the manufacture of locomotives. The Northern, North Eastern, and Southern. The Northern Division's headquarters were at Crewe, the works formerly of the Grand Junction Railway. Francis Trevithick the son of the famous Richard Trevithick of 'Pennydarren' fame was appointed superintendent with Alexander Allen as works manager. The North Eastern Division was situated at Longsight formerly of the Manchester & Birmingham Railway. In 1857 this division was absorbed into the Northern Division and at this time Trevithick retired and was replaced by John Ramsbottom as superintendent 1851–1871. The headquarters of the Southern Division was at Wolverton formerly of the London & Birmingham Railway. Edward Bury was superintendent and it's where he designed the 'Bury' 2-2-0 passenger engine. He resigned in 1847 and was replaced by James McConnell. There were significant differences between the Northern and Southern Divisions locomotive policies. Crewe from its foundation in 1843 built engines, whereas at Wolverton in 1838 the set up was mainly for repair work with engines bought from outside manufacturers. From 1845 to 1855 only a dozen engines were built, however this increased substantially from 1856. In 1862 after a disagreement over costs McConnell resigned and both the Northern and Southern Divisions were amalgamated with John Ramsbottom becoming overall locomotive superintendent By 1865 all engine manufacture was based at Crewe, with Wolverton becoming the L.N.W.R. carriage works.

Trevithick small firebox 6ft. dw. 2-2-2 'Crewe Type' built pre 1853. Photographed 1875

Edward Talbot collection

The livery colours of engines of both divisions were green, however when McConnell took over at Wolverton the livery of that division was changed to vermilion red. Once the two divisions were amalgamated and Francis Webb became overall superintendent replacing Ramsbottom when he retired a universal colour of 'Blackberry Black' was introduced for all locomotives.

Early Engines of the Irish Mail
The early L.N.W.R. engines built at Crewe by Superintendent Francis Trevithick were known as 'Crewe Types', however this is somewhat misleading as the design was not created at the Crewe works though production was carried out there from 1843 to 1857. The design was attributed to Alexander Allen who became works manager but there seems to be some speculation about other third party participation as to this fact. Though this is mere supposition, and open to debate and without any clarification Allen must be given the credit for the design.
*** The engines were the 5ft. 6inch. driving wheel 2-2-2 passenger singles and the 5ft. dw. 2-4-0 Goods type with outside cylinders. The main inside iron plate frame extended the full length of the engine and carried the driving and coupled axle boxes. In addition there were also an outside iron plate frame which took the two 2-2-2 or the one 2-4-0 carrying axle boxes on each side. The sloping cylinders were situated between the inside and outside frames and were secured to both. The 'Crewe Type' did not extend any further than these wheel arrangements.

There were also three experimental engines built in 1847 the 8ft. 6inch. dw. 2-2-2 No. 173 Cornwall, the 7ft. dw. 4-2-0 Crampton type rear drive No. 176 Courier, and the 7ft. dw. 2-2-2 No. 187 Velocipede. These engines were used for the Irish Mail but with speed and reliability being the

7ft. dw. 2-2-2 'Pegasus' No. 1840 after rebuilding to 'Raven Class'
in 1865. Originally built in 1853 as No. 31.
Worked the Irish Mail from Holyhead to Chester
Edward Talbot collection

Experimental engine 8ft. 6inch. dw 2-2-2 No 173 'Cornwall'
Rebuilt by John Ramsbottom to 'Crewe Tyep' 1858
Edward Talbot collection

utmost of requirements complaints from the C&H Rly. to the L.N.W.R. regarding insufficient power of the engines for mail duties resulted in a request being made to the L.N.W.R. for more competent engines.

Courier was withdrawn from service in 1854 and was sold to the Royal Swedish Railway. Velocipede underwent two rebuilds in 1860 and 1869 to 'Ravenclass' standard. *** 'The Crewe Type' D.H.Stuart & B.Reed Pg.49 Cornwall was also rebuilt in 1858 with an overslung boiler to 'Ravenclass' and underwent further rebuilding in 1871 and 1877.

Replacements for the C&H Rly. section of the Irish Mail route were introduced by the L.N.W.R. with the Ravenclass of engine. The 7ft. dw. 2-2-2 No. 31 Pegasus and No. 18 Cerberus built at Crewe in 1853 and 1857 respectively were stationed at Holyhead, they were later rebuilt in1865 and 1869. The prototype of the 7ft. dw. 2-2-2 single, No. 290 Rocket built at Crewe in 1852, later rebuilt in 1864, and No. 187 rebuilt Velocipede were stationed at Chester. These four engines worked the Irish mail until replaced by the 'Problem' class of engine, sixty of which were built at Crewe. The first in 1859 was the 7ft. 6inch. dw. 2-2-2 No. 184 Problem (works No. 424). All had open footplates, cabs were not added until the 1870's, and further rebuilding took place in the 1890's. One of the class was No. 531 Lady of the Lake which was awarded a bronze medal at the

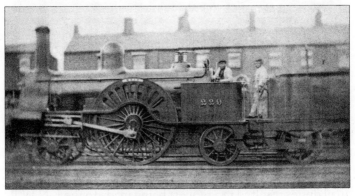

Problem Class 7ft. 6inch. dw. 2-2-2 No. 229 'Watt'
Photograph showing height of the side of tender compared to the engine cab side. Indicating a water capacity of 2000 gallons, which was introduced by Ramsbottom. Previously tenders were of 1500 gallons capacity.

Edward Talbot collection

Unidentified 2-2-2 Problem Class piloting a 2-2-2 compound with
the Up day mail.
After leaving the Tubular bridge at Conway

Loc. & General Office collection
Courtesy L.N.W.R. Society

International exhibition in London in 1862 and from then
on this class of engine was referred to as the 'Lady of the
Lake' class. The tenders of which had a water carrying
capacity of 2000 gallons necessary for the long haul working
of the Irish Mail, carried out by Northern Division engines
which by then were working from Holyhead to as far as
Stafford. One particular feature of this class of engine was
that they were fitted with a water pick up apparatus, as
mentioned in the previous chapter. Also incorporated in the
design of the engines were the usual Ramsbottom features
of safety valves, screw reverser, horizontal smoke box door
and distinctive design of the chimney top. They were a very
reliable engine but it was said that they did have an unusual
lateral movement when running at full speed, also there was
a tendency being a 'single' with a large driving wheel to
labour somewhat when accounting head on gale force winds
across the North Wales coast and Anglesey. The Problem
locomotives worked the Irish Mail service until the late

1870's. when they were replaced by the 2-4-0 Newton's and 2-4-0 Precedent Classes. They went on to do useful work as pilots for heavier engines requiring an assistant engine, before the 'Class' was eventually scrapped by 1907.

Initially the engines of the Southern Division that worked the Irish Mail were mainly the 'Jenny Lind' class, a 6ft. dw 2-2-2 designed by David Jay and built by E. B. Wilson & Co. Leeds of which two are recorded in the L.N.W.R. (S.Div.) list, works No.'s 208, 209, (L.N.W. No.'s 808, 809.) and also six 6ft. 6inch. dw. 2-2-2 built by Bury, Curtis & Kennedy, works No.'s. 12, 18, 65, 67, 75, 218, (L.N.W. No.'s 612, 618, 665, 667, 675, 818.). These were eventually replaced in 1851 by McConnell's designed 7ft. dw. 2-2-2 singles, forty of which were by built by Sharp Bros. (later Sharp Stewart & Co. (25), Kilson & Co. (5). and Wolverton works (10). The first of this class was works No. 247, (L.N.W No. 847) and named 'Odin' in 1872. All were characterised by large boilers and had all the bearings inside thereby exposing all their wheels. This led to them being nicknamed 'Bloomers', at a time that Mrs Amelia Bloomer

McConnell 'Southern Division' 'Small Bloomer' 6ft. 6inch. dw. 2-2-2 Worked the Irish Mail from London to Stafford
Courtesy Edward Talbot collection

was advocating certain startling changes in Victorian attire. Like the Problem class of the Northern Division the Bloomers worked the Irish Mail as far as Stafford.

Eventually as larger and higher performance engines were developed the necessity to change engines at Stafford ceased with engines having the capacity to work the whole route from London to Holyhead.

L.N.W.R. Express Passenger Engines From 1870–1920
Abbreviations
DW. Driving Wheel.
WB.eng. Wheelbase of Engine.
TL. Total Length over Buffers Engine & Tender.
EW. Engine Weight.
W.eng&tdr. fl. Weight of Engine and Tender fully laden.
TC. Tender Capacity.
CC. Coal Capacity
( ) Amount Built

Locomotive Superintendent J. Ramsbottom 1857–1871

Samson Class 2-4-0
Built 1863–79 (90)
DW. 6ft.
EW. 26tons 2cwt.

Newton Class 2-4-0
Built 1866–73 (96)
DW. 6ft.
WB.eng. 15ft. 8inch.
TL. Engine only 26ft.
EW. 29tons

Francis Webb 1871–1903
Precursor Class 2-4-0
Built 1874–79 (40)
DW. 5ft. 6inch.
WB. eng. 15ft. 8inch.
TL. Engine only 23ft. 9inch.

Precedent Class 2-4-0
Built 1875–82 (70)
DW. 6ft. 6inch.
WB.eng. 15ft. 8inch.
TL. 46ft. 10¾inch.

EW. 60tons 12cwt.
Counterparts of 5 ft. 6inch.
Precursors
62 renewed & 8 rebuilt as
Renewed

Renewed Precedent Class 2-4-0 1P

Built 1887–1901 (166)
  incl. Newton's and
  Precedents.
DW. 6ft. 3inch.
WB.eng. 15ft. 8inch.
TL. 46ft. 10¾inch.
W.eng&tdr.fl. 60tons 12cwt.
TC. 1800gallons.
CC. 4½tons

Jubilee Class 4-4-0 2P

Four Cylinder Compound.
Built1899–1900 (38)

DW. 7ft. 1inch.
WB.eng. 23ft. 2inch.
TL. 53ft. 9½inch.
W.eng&tdr.fl. 86tons
TC. 2500gallons.
CC. 5tons.
These engines were used on the heaviest fastest trains and had 9ft. 8inch. coupling rods the longest in the country at the time

Alfred the Great Class 4-4-0 2P

Four Cylinder Compound
Built 1901–03 (40)
DW. 7ft. 1inch.
WB.eng. 23ft. 3inch.
TL. 54ft. 8inch.
W.eng&tdr.fl. 94tons 12cwt.
TC. 3000gallons
CC. 5tons
A development of the 'Jubilee' class, but with a larger boiler. They superseded the Jubilee on the heaviest express trains.

George Whale 1903–1909

Precursor Class 4-4-0 2P/3P	Experiment Class 4-6-0 3P
Built 1904–07 (130)	Built 1905–10 (105)
DW. 6ft. 9inch.	DW. 6ft. 3inch.
WB.eng. 25ft. 1½ inch.	WB. eng. 26ft. 8½ inch.
TL. 56ft. 2inch.	TL. 57ft. 3½ inch.
W.eng&tdr.fl. 96tons 15cwt.	W.eng&tdr.fl. 102tons 15cwt.
TC. 3000gallons	TC. 3000gallons

Renown Class 4-4-0 2P
Built 1908–24 (70)
DW. 7ft. 1inch.
WB.eng. 23ft. 2inch.
TL. 52ft. 0½ inch.
W.eng&tdr.fl. 81tons 7cwt.
TC. 2000gallons
CC. 5tons
Simple rebuilds of Jubilee and Alfred the Great Classes.

Charles John Bowen Cooke 1909–20

George V Class 4-4-0 2P	Queen Mary Class 4-4-0
Built 1910–1 (90)	Built 1910 (10)
Superheated	
DW. 6ft. 9inch.	DW. 6ft. 9inch.
WB. eng. 25ft. 1½inch.	All later converted to George V Class

Prince of Wales Class 4-6-0 3P	Claughton Class 4-6-0 5P
Built 1911–22 (245)	Built 1913–21 (130)
Superheated	Superheated
DW. 6ft. 3inch.	DW. 6ft. 6inch.
WB.eng. 26ft. 8½inch.	TL. 63ft. 4¾inch.

TL. 57ft. 9inch.
W.eng&tdr. fl. 103tons
TC. 3000gallons
CC. 6tons

W.eng&tdr. fl. 117tons
TC. 3000gallons
CC. 6tons
Four Cylinders two inside and
two outside.

*4-4-0 Renown Class No. 1968 'Cumberland piloting a George Class
No. 2197 'Planet'*
Passing through Bangor station with an 'Up Day Irish Mail'
Courtesy of L.N.W.R. Society
L.N.W.R.S. General photos

George V Class 4-4-0 L.N.W.R. No. 2106 'Holyhead'
L.M.S. No. 5408
Built at Crewe July 1915 No. 5245
Superheated version of the 'Precursor Class'
Withdrawn from service May 1937
Edward Talbot collection

Chapter 10

1860 to 1920

The Abergele Disaster

Thursday 20th August 1868

On the morning of the 20th August a goods train left Crewe for Holyhead, at Saltney Wharf two wagons containing 50 casks of paraffin oil were attached to the rear of the train in front of the guards brake van. The train arrived at Abergele at 12.15pm where some shunting of the wagons was carried out. Departing Abergele it arrived at Llandulas at 12.24pm with a load of 17 loaded and 26 empty wagons including those loaded with paraffin which were still positioned at the rear of the train. On arrival at Llandulas where there were two sidings just east of the platform, the goods train entered into the sidings to clear the main line in readiness for the down Irish Mail due at 12.39pm. Unfortunately there were other wagons in both sidings which did not afford room for the whole train. Shunting therefore of the train in stages had to be carried out so that all the wagons could be dispersed into the sidings thereby leaving the main line clear. However a decision was taken to uncouple the rear six wagons and the brake van of the train and leave them on the main line with only the brakes engaged on the brake van. The brakes on the other wagons were left off. The remainder of the train was pulled forward into the sidings clear of the points where fly shunting of wagons was carried out to make way for those on the main line. Unbelievably a loaded timber wagon with check wagons at either side was mistakenly shunted towards the stationary wagons on the main line, the three wagons struck the vehicles with such force that it broke the cog wheel on the brakes of the brake van, simultaneously all ten wagons on the main line slowly gained momentum down the 1 in 100 gradient coming up from Abergele. Although attempts were made to try and stop the wagons they outrun those chasing them. The runaway wagons continued down the track, and round a bend into the path of the oncoming Irish Mail travelling at 40mph (64kmph) which resulted in a dreadful disaster.

The 'Mail' had left Chester at 11.48am having taken on four extra carriages at the front of the train. The driver of the 'Mail' Arthur Thompson when he spotted the runaways immediately shut off steam and reversed the engine whilst his fireman Joseph Holmes tended to the brakes. Seeing that no more could be done the driver shouted to his mate to jump clear. Whilst the driver managed to jump clear fireman Holmes was too late, the train ploughed into the runaway wagons. On impact the engine, tender, and leading guards van were derailed with the engine overturning to the left, and the tender overturning to the right blocking the UP main line. Immediately the engine, tender, front guards van and three front carriages were engulfed in an inferno of fire, the impact of the crash had shattered the paraffin casks, scattering the fuel over the front of the train which subsequently ignited. A fourth carriage then also caught fire along with the front of the travelling post office. The guard in the rear guards van who was injured, had the presence of mind to inform one of the surviving passengers to run to Llandulas station which was a mile away to warn of the accident and to close the UP line to traffic. Immediate help came from workers at a local quarry as well as farm labourers from the adjoining fields who tried to extinguish the fire by forming a bucket chain to fetch water from the nearby sea.

In all thirty three victims perished in the conflagration, which included all passengers in the first four carriages, the guard in the front guards van and the fireman. Identification of the bodies was impossible due to them being burnt beyond recognition, apart from three who were identified by their personal effects. One was ***Lord Farnham who was identified by the crest engraved on his watch. There were no serious casualties in the carriages behind the post van. In his book the Chester and Holyhead Railway the author J. M. Dunn. refers to a book by Lord Frederick Hamilton 'the Days before Yesterday' who was eleven at the time of the accident describing the action of his eldest brother the Marquis of Hamilton another survivor who with the help of other passengers uncoupled the undamaged carriages and being on an incline they rolled clear of the fire. Eventually an engine arrived at the scene and both the carriages and survivors were taken back to Abergele.

Extract from the report in the *North Wales Chronicle* 29 August 1868:

> *'According to all accounts the front of the carriages of the train were on fire a few seconds after the collision and they were enveloped in a mass of flame.*
>
> *One of the passengers who escaped from a carriage at the rear of the train thus described the scene.*
>
> *For an hour the fire continued to burn without any sign of abatement. The carriages were literally one burning mass and the liquid fire running over the surface of the ground charred and blackened everything with which came into contact.'*

At the crash site railway gangs that had been called worked intensely to clear the wreckage and repair the track before the night mails came through and also had the unenviable task of recovering the remains of the victims who were placed in coffins marked with just numbers. The

2-2-2 Problem Class No. 291 'Prince of Wales'
This was the engine in the Abergele Disaster, built 1862, repaired
after crash, and scrapped 1906

Norman Lee's collection
Courtesy L.N.W.R. Society

engine Problem Class No. 291 'Prince of Wales' was eventually salvaged, repaired and remained in service until it was scrapped in 1906.

Following a Board of Trade inquiry headed by Col. Rich it was concluded that as it was there seemed to be a particular malaise on behalf of the railway company when it came to enforcing safety regulations. At a subsequent inquest the jury severely censured the stationmaster, and returned a verdict of manslaughter against the two brakesmen of the goods train for their actions in not securing the wagons correctly and for the non observance of the rule of the company which requires that all goods trains must be shunted at stations or sidings at least before any passenger train is due. The Board of Trade inquiry also brought to light that there was no applicable regulations as to the conveyance of dangerous goods and also that some of the doors of the mail carriages had been locked, both practices of which were censured by Col. Rich.

Monument in St Michael's Church yard Abergele erected to the memory of the Thirty Three passengers buried there who perished in the Irish Mail Disaster 20th August 1868.

Author's collection

Rt. Hon. Henry Ford Farnham

The Lady Farnham

The Rev. Sir Nichols Chinnery

Lady Chinnery

The Hon. Judge Berwick

Elizabeth Berwick

John Harrison Aylmer

Rosanna Louisa Aylmer

Arthur Fitzgerald Aylmer

Rosalie Franks

Katie Sophia Askin

Fanny Sophia Thorburg Askin

Charles Gripps

Capt. J. Priestly Edwards

Priestly Augustus Edwards

E. Lowell Farrell

Joseph Holmes

Jane Ingram

Mary Ann Kellet

Caroline Simcox Lea

Augusta Simcox Lea

William Townsend Lund

W. Henry Owen

Edward Outen

W. Bradley Parkinson

Christopher Slater Parkinson

Mary An Roe

Whitmore Scovell

Kathleen Scovell

William Smith

Caroline Stearn

Elizabeth Strafford

Louisa Symes

It was finally concluded that if the brakes on the wagons that were on the main line had been correctly locked and the distant signal set then the accident could have been avoided, therefore there needed to an improved means of communication along the line.

The victims of the crash were eventually interred in a mass grave in Abergele

***Footnote: Henry Maxwell 7th Baron Farnham b. 1799 d. 1868.
House of Commons M.P. for County Caven 1824–1838. House of Lords Irish Peer 1839–1868
Married Anna Stapleton daughter of Thomas Stapleton 16th Baron le Despencer 3rd. Dec. 1828.
No children.

Churchyard and a cross was placed by the rail side at the site of the accident in Memoriam, this was later replaced by an inscribed slate stone. Driver Thompson suffered serious injuries which led to his death in October1868.

The two brakesmen were sent for trial at Ruthin assizes but were acquitted.

Account of Alfred Sara driver of the goods train at the inquiry of the disaster as reported by the *North Wales Chronicle* 5th August 1868:

'The train I drive is called the 'pick up' train. We are timed to shunt the at Llandulas for the Irish Mail to pass. We generally shunt at the siding there. If we have not time to get there we shunt at Abergele or sometimes at Rhyl. On the Thursday in question we intended to shunt at Llandulas the usual place. We had wagons both to leave there and take up there. The siding is under the control of the stationmaster at Llandulas. He worked the signals there. He was on duty on this Thursday. Sometimes he orders his son to work the signals. I am not certain who worked the signals on that day,

but I saw the stationmaster there. The danger signal was put as soon as I arrived. That is the usual course taken when we are going to shunt the train into the siding. A portion of the train was shunted into the siding, because there was not enough room for the whole of it. If there had been room we should have shunted the whole of it into the siding. I could not on my accord have shunted the train into the siding. I have to take my orders from the brakesmen. Both the brakesmen that day gave me orders respecting that shunt. They were given by signal as I was drawing up. I brought up the locomotive fast to the end of Llandulas station and opposite the signal. The break van and two wagons next to it would be clear at the points in connection with the siding. I then got a signal from the brakesman I believe go ahead. I went ahead and found that a portion of the tail end of the train was left standing on the line. I do not know who unhooked it. I should say it stood for 10 minutes. The tail end of the train consisted of the brake van, two paraffin wagons and one other wagon or more; but what it contained I do not know. They were loaded. I then received a signal to stop so I did. I afterwards received a signal to back. The stationmaster was holding the points and I fly shunted, ten or twelve waggons into the siding and kept the remainder on the line. Having got the waggons into the siding the signal given to me to come back. I backed a few yards, when I got the signal to stop and noticed there were loaded waggons parted from the train going backwards towards the rear end of the train which had been left on the main line. It was the brakesman who had unhooked those three wagons from the train. This place is on an incline towards Abergele. I should have thought these wagons would have gone down the incline by their own weight without any backing from the train. Having backed I brought the train to a standstill. I was again sent ahead by a signal from the brakesman and was stopped by his signal. I received another signal to come back into the siding. I backed for the purpose of leaving some more wagons in the sidings and of pushing the wagons already in the siding as far as it would go into it, in order to make room for shunting the whole train into the siding so as to leave room for the Irish Mail.

While I was doing this, I saw three trucks which had been parted from the train moving down the incline. They had not reached the tail end of the train that had been left on the main line. I had not seen any person putting a break on them. I saw the two brakesmen running after them but neither of them overtook them. I did not see the trucks strike the tail end of the train because they went round the curve out of my sight.

I did not look at my watch but as nearly as I can say it would be from twenty to twenty five past twelve o'clock when we arrived at Llandulas station. It would be about twelve thirty five when I saw the three wagons start off. The Irish Mail is not time tabled for Llandulas, but is due at Abergele at twelve thirty four. Llandulas is 3½ miles from Abergele'.

The Tamworth Accident

September 14th 1870

The station at Tamworth had four lines running through it, two up and two down lines. The two central lines were for through main line traffic whilst the two outer lines were loop lines to the platforms used for stopping of goods and passenger trains. Connecting to the east up line were points that led to a siding 150yds. (136.5mtrs.) in length with a buffer stop at the end. The approach to the station from the north the view was somewhat restricted by two bridges the *** Board of Trade Report

Gungate bridge and Mace's bridge and a curve in the line through a deep cutting. Protection of the line was afforded by a distant, intermediate, and a home signal. Controlling the four lines were two signal boxes north and south of the station set on the main line, the means of communication between the two was by bell, one ring for a through train and two for a platform train, acknowledgment of receiving the bell was by a disc display receiver set in the signalbox. Also there was a further bridge above and over the station that carried the Midland Railway line.

*** The Irish Mail consisting of the following marshalling, with a total weight of 133 Tons

Engine and Tender
Guard's Brake van
Composite carriage
Post Office
and tender
Luggage van
Composite carriage
Composite   "
Composite   "
1st. Class   "
1st. Class   "
Guard's Brake van

Departed Holyhead 18 minutes late at 12.13am due to the late arrival of the mail steamer from Kingstown, stopping at Chester, and passing through Crewe it arrived at Stafford at 3.33am and after changing engines left at 3.37am 14 minutes late. It approached Tamworth at 4.9am 13 minutes late.

The South box signal man had set the main line clear in readiness for the 'mail' thereby isolating the south loop of the platform line. However the points from the platform line *** Board of Trade Report to the siding were left open. The North box signalman was expecting a Manchester goods train and had set the signals and points for the loop line in readiness for it to clear the main line ahead of the Irish Mail. After checking his watch which showed 3.50am he saw a white light coming out from under the bridge to the north of the box, and on hearing no whistle, he determined that it must be a light engine as the goods train would have displayed a green light. Further checking his watch he realised that it had stopped at 3.50am, and the train approaching was the Irish Mail, he immediately reversed the signals to danger but it was to late, the mail train had already passed them on clear and was travelling at 45mph, then due to the line being set for the goods train it crossed over the points to platform loop line. On realising the mistake the driver of the 'mail' applied the brakes and sounded a series of alarm whistles to alert the guards in the front and rear brake vans for them to apply the brakes there. The train passed through the station and into the sidings with it speed reduced to about 15mph it crashed through the stop end buffers and finally ended up in the river Anker flowing close by. The engine remained upright but at right angles to the line, the tender fell on its side also at right angles, the front brake van was completely shattered and the following seven carriages were seriously damaged. Fortunately the two 1st Class carriages and rear brake van remained upright on the line. Tragically the driver, fireman and one passenger were killed and thirteen were injured, which included the guard in the front brake van.

Based on a report by Mr H. W. Tyler Secretary (Railway Dept.) Board of Trade. 'The following is a condensed version of his conclusions into the accident.'

1. The primary cause of the accident was the misdirection of the train to the platform line.
2. Insufficient warning to the driver that the points were set incorrectly.

3. Lateness of the goods train which accounted for long expectation on behalf of the north signalman.

4. The incompleteness of locking arrangements with to the plan of the station and the conditions of the traffic, also both signalmen acted independently of each other regarding the arrangement.

The following Memorandum was issued on 9 November 1869 to Tamworth up and down signalmen.

'On receiving two beats of the bell, to indicate a train approaching that is to stop at the station, let the signalman on duty at the other end at once set his loop points for the main line, so that should the train overshoot the platform, it will run out upon the main line, and not risk running into any wagons that may be standing in the siding.'

5. The working practices that were employed at the time were not desirable, in that leaving the distant and intermediate signals at clear, whilst the home signal and points were set for the platform line. The safer practice would be to keep the points clear for the through line and

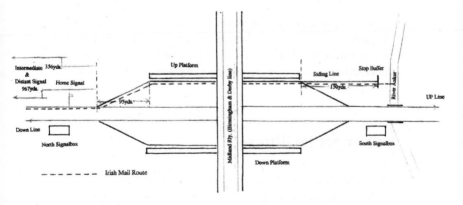

Lay out of Tamworth Station, 14th September 1870
Representative Drawing Based on Accident Report

Author collection

only alter them on the actual approach of a stopping train.

6. It was clear that there was adequate brake power on the train, but the condition of the rails raised doubts, in that the siding rails which were in a greasy condition could have compromised the brake power of the train.

7. That a standard issue clock should be made available, without signalmen relying on their own time pieces.

8. The introduction of the electric telegraph system of control which was being incorporated along the railway network to give ample warning of trains had not come into operation in the signalboxes at Tamworth. Although the instruments were in place they had only been used by day for practicing and were not functional. Therefore the signalmen had no contact with other boxes up and down the line. However the telegraph system was in place at Tamworth station and notice there was given of the approach of the Irish Mail but it was not communicated to the signalboxes. As a consequence had the information been passed on appropriate action could have avoided the accident.

Footnote: It is apparent that before the introduction of the electric telegraph system of control, journey by rail was of a precarious and perilous nature, which relied basically on the fallibility of the time table and expectation and observance of the signalmen, which left with little room for error.

Passenger facilities

The introduction of sleeping cars on the Irish Mail was made on the 1st March 1875 for first class passengers only. They were very basic, and a far cry from those of today's standard. Comprising of a compartment for Ladies and two for Gentlemen. They had day seats with roof hammock beds, which made up into four sleeping berths. Seats in the compartments were bookable both in Euston and Holyhead at a charge of five shillings (25p).

Another facility that became available was the introduction in 1876 of luncheon baskets at Chester which added considerably to the comfort of passengers. There were two choices available, one an up market basket at five shillings (25p) and an ordinary basket at two shillings and sixpence (12½ p).

*** 5/-	2/6
Pint of Claret or ½ Pint of Sherry	Pint of Ale or Stout
Chicken, Ham or Tongue	Cold Meat or Pie
Butter, Cheese and Bread	Cheese and Bread

*** Neale Railway Reminiscences Pg 243

Restaurant Cars were not introduced until 1895 when on the day mail breakfast and luncheon were provided on the 'up' mail, and luncheon and tea on the 'down' mail.

In 1897 Third Class passengers were admitted on the mail trains.

The building of the Holyhead Breakwater and Harbour of Refuge

With the construction of the railway to Holyhead it was anticipated that the port would see a significant increase in shipping. Also Holyhead was ideal, geographically located between the St. George's Channel and the North Irish Sea, and presented itself as perfect place of refuge for all shipping. The Government therefore made a decision to construct an outer harbour of refuge by means of a breakwater.

Plans were submitted by four eminent engineers of the time. Mr J. M. Rendell, Mr J. Walker, Capt. Beechey RN.

*View of the
breakwater taken
from Holyhead
Mountain*
Roy Davies

and Capt. H. Evans, of which Mr Rendell was successful, an engineer with a wealth of experience having been involved in various projects throughout the country. He was born in Devon in 1799, and in his early years worked as a young surveyor under Thomas Telford making surveys for the proposed suspension bridge across the river Mersey at Runcorn. Other projects he was involved with were the plans for the Birkenhead docks and construction of the docks at Grimsby. In 1836 he designed the plans for Brixham Harbour, and breakwater at Torquay and in 1837 designed the Mill Bay Pier near Plymouth a project of similar nature to the Holyhead breakwater.

In 1845 Rendell provided detailed plans to the Lords of the Treasury and Royal assent was given in an act of Parliament in July 1847.

The plan was for the construction of two breakwaters in Holyhead Bay. One the North breakwater of 5360ft. in length, firstly heading 1450ft. approx. N.E from an area known as Soldiers Point and then 3920ft. approx. due East. The other breakwater 2000ft. in length heading north from an area called Salt Island. This is where the packet port of the Admiralty Pier was situated. The overall construction gave an enclosed area of water of 320 acres.

Rendell's resident engineer was George C. Dobson and the contract for the work was signed on the 24th December

1847 which was awarded to J. and C. Rigby brothers of London.

It was planned that the level of the sea bed be raised to the high water mark by means of a rock foundation some 250ft. wide, on this the structure of the breakwater itself was to be built. The source of the rock required was to be quarried from the Holyhead mountain which stands some 700 to 800ft. above sea level being adjacent to the proposed site of the construction.

Preparatory work commenced in January 1848 which included the building of two 7ft. 0¼ broad gauge railways which were contemporary to 'Brunels' broad gauge Great Western Railway at the time, these were laid from the quarry to the site of the North and East breakwaters respectively, along with workshops, offices, saw mills, and all other necessary requirements for the work ahead, which included magazines for the storage of black powder required for the blasting of rock.

Construction began in 1849 which required a constant workforce of 1300 men. Also needed were eight railway engines, fifty cranes, and 250 large iron tilting tip wagons designed by Dobson and capable of carrying 8 to 10 tons of stone.

The method of construction was by means of a staging of wooden piles 18inch. square and 80ft. in length supported by A frames made of Quebec pine timber which were erected into the sea 17ft. above high water. Boxes were constructed and attached to the piles and filled with stones to add stability. The staging was 150ft. wide and carried five railway lines. Loaded wagons were pulled forward and tipped sideways emptying their cargoes of stone between the gaps in the staging and into the sea, thus forming the breakwaters foundation. Positioned at the head of the staging were two cranes assisted by a small steamer which were employed in positioning new piles in advance of the construction work behind.

Sadly Rendell died in London on the 21st November 1856 of a fever and was replaced by civil engineer John Hawkshaw who remained to complete the project.

Although work on the East breakwater had begun it was brought to a halt in 1856 by a change of plan, when it was felt that that the second breakwater would make the entrance to the harbour to small, also the position of the submerged Platters Rocks running on a line NW from Salt Island and SSE from the proposed end of the North breakwater would be a hazard to shipping. After debate with the engineers Capt. Skinner the Harbour master (nephew of the renowned Capt. John Macgregor Skinner) wrote to the Admiralty urging them to consider enlarging the Harbour by extending the North breakwater by 2000ft. in a NE direction This was agreed to, along with a further extension of 500ft. increasing the total length of the breakwater to 7860ft. long (1.48 miles). Thereby giving a further deep water anchorage of 400 acres and a total anchorage in all of 720 acres. In consequence the Admiralty Pier area for the mail packet ships would be left exempt from vessels seeking refuge.

Note: Measurements taken from the Admiralty Chart of 22nd August 1881 by Capt. Sir Frederick J. Evans, shows the breakwater as 7390ft. (Ynys Mon County Archives)
As a layman Author's personal survey 7956ft.

The structure of the breakwater was built of quartzite rock some of which were 15 tons in weight which had been extracted from the quarry on the mountain. The parapets, paving, etc. were comprised of limestone quarried from the Moelfre quarry on the north coast of Anglesey. This was shipped into the site of the abandoned East breakwater on Salt Island where it was loaded on to railway wagons for transportation by the broad gauge railway to the North breakwater.

The breakwater itself 57ft. 3inch. in diameter was built in two tiers or terraces which are connected by steps placed at intervals along its length. Further to this alcoves were built into the wall of the top tier on the inner harbour side for use as shelter out of the elements. The end section or Head of the breakwater 150ft. long by 50ft. wide was built of massive square stones, with divers laying the masonry below the water line. Constructed on this section was a square designed 70ft. lighthouse which showed a red light, the design in the main was to accommodate a more comfortable living space for the lightkeepers.

The breakwater was finally completed in June of 1873 at a cost of £1,285,000. It took twenty eight years to build from the planning stage to completion and used 7 million tons of rock in its construction. Unfortunately accidents were a regular occurrence and tragically fatalities were substantial. In one period alone from 1849–52 over 40 lives were lost.

On Tuesday 19th August 1873 Edward Prince of Wales arrived by Royal Yacht and travelled to the head of the breakwater via the quarry railway and ceremoniously declared the work complete.

There had been one other Royal visit during the construction when in 1853 Queen Victoria, Prince Albert, and other members of the Royal Family when on a visit to the breakwater and quarry witnessed the detonation of 400lb of explosives which brought down 20,000tons of rock. At this time the foundation of the breakwater was 4000ft. into the bay.

On completion of the Breakwater one rail line and one engine named the 'Prince Albert' were retained by the Board of Trade to carry out any necessary repair and maintenance. The engine remained in service until 1913 when the line was changed to that of Standard Gauge 4ft. 8½inch.

Dimensions of the Breakwater
Length 7860ft. (1.48 miles) (2.37km)
Width 57ft. 3ins. (17.5m)
Top of the breakwater is 27ft. above the High Water Mark (8.2m)
Width of the top tier or terrace 14ft. 3ins. (4.3m)
Width of the bottom tier or quay 40ft. (12.3m)
Height between the two tiers 12ft. (3.69)
Height of parapet 4ft. (1.2m)

It is interesting to note that prior to the commencement to the Breakwater project in 1848 earlier plans had been drawn up by Mr J. M. Rendell of a totally different concept for the Outer Harbour. In a report of 5th December 1845 he submitted plans and recommendations for a Packet port and Refuge Harbour to the Government which included a breakwater and two internal piers with berthing facilities also laid out was the building of a railway station in the vicinity of the Admiralty Pier. It was anticipated the construction would take seven years at a cost of £628,063. The other main contributor to the project was the Chester and Holyhead Rly. Co. with an expected required investment of £200,000. As a temporary accommodation during construction Rendell proposed the dredging and deepening of the Admiralty pier area and the building of three new jetties at a cost of £16,500.

In general the whole scheme was controversial which brought a response in a very comprehensive document styled letter from Charles Williams Esq. of Liverpool

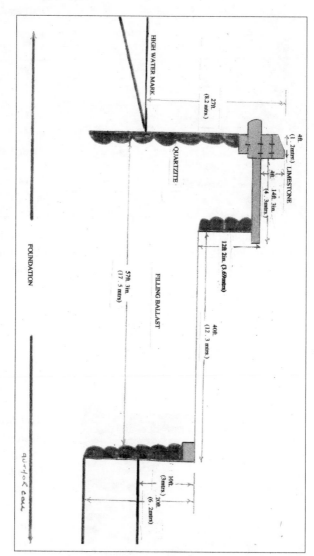

The Breakwater (Cross Section)

Author's collection

Photograph of the leeward side of the upper terrace of the break water showing the extent of the size of rocks used in its construction

Author's collection

Holyhead Breakwater. Showing the North facing seaward side with the sea at the high water level. Projecting from the sea are remnants of the Quebec wooden pilings used in the construction

Author's collection

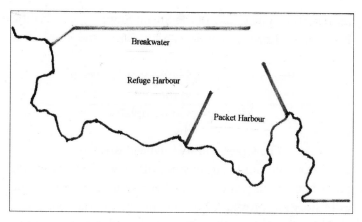

Drawing showing a basic depiction of the Breakwater based on a proposed plan submitted by J. M. Rendall C.E. 1845

Author collection
Courtesy Ynys Môn Archives

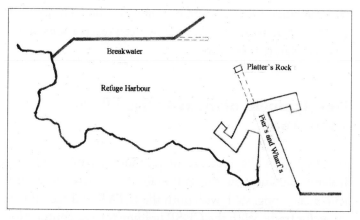

Drawing showing a basic depiction of the Breakwater based on a proposed plan submitted by J. M. Rendall C.E. 1850

Author collection
Courtesy Ynys Môn Archives

representing The Office of the Steam Shipping Association London to Lord Viscount Sandon M.P. and headed as follows:

Proposed Asylum Harbour at Holyhead

and the

Monopoly Contemplated

by

The Chester and Holyhead Rly. Co.

The letter laid out his misgivings of the whole undertaking and whether this prompted further inquiry is uncertain, but as History has proved the project never materialised.

However before the alterations to the design of the breakwater in1856, another plan by Mr I. M. Rendell had been drafted in 1850 titled 'The New Harbour of Holyhead'. Although it contained an outline of the original plan it showed significant changes. A reduction in length of the North breakwater but with a construction to the N.E. Also shown was a reduction to the East breakwater with a more substantial structure projecting from Salt Island, which included wharves and berthing facilities. Therefore it questions had there already in 1850 been reservations of the original planned structure.

Development of the Holyhead Port 1860–1880

By 1860 with the increase in rail and steamer traffic to Ireland, facilities on the Admiralty Pier were becoming somewhat congested, with both the LNWR and CDSP Co. vying for trade. With the CDSP holding the sea contract for the conveyance of mails and the LNWR holding the land mail contract along with express passenger traffic for their own ships, the Board of the LNWR realised that the only possible solution was to develop an inner harbour to provide facilities for both its rail and sea passengers to such a standard which would eventually bring them the much sought after sea mail contract. This would require extending and deepening the existing tidal creek as it was then from Salt Island to their railway station situated along the town side of the harbour.

Through an act of parliament of 1861 authority was given to purchase land for the construction of an embankment on the north west side to replace the timber extension line from the station to the Admiralty Pier. Also in 1863 the LNWR were given a ninety nine year lease by the Board of Trade for land on the west side of the inner harbour giving access to the station, eventually in an act of 1869 the railway company were given the opportunity to purchase the freehold of the lands leased by the Board Of Trade.

The contract for the improvements were awarded to Messrs J & C Rigby in May 1863 the same contractors that were engaged in the breakwater project. The work involved building a coffer dam across the mouth of the harbour, and eight hundred men were employed in deepening the old creek basin, the excavated material of which was deposited on the East side of the creek thereby filling in the coves that were situated in that area. There was also construction of a new quay for berthing facilities, building a goods shed 750ft. long by 41ft. wide, offices, marine workshops, and rail sidings capable of marshalling carriages and 512 wagons, and also a diversion of the mail train line to the Admiralty Pier, being to the west of the goods warehouse, also a road named Admiralty Road, known today as Victoria Rd. A further requirement was the enlargement of the station, and the diversion of the A5 road by a bridge over the railway replacing the then level crossing. A cattle lairage and sidings with capability for 159 cattle wagons was also built south of the station at the site of the temporary station built in 1848 with a connecting over rail road from the quay side.

At this time a wooden pier 460ft. (140mtrs.) long was built as an extension to the Admiralty pier, which ensured a deep water berth at all tides.

The dredging work of deepening the harbour was completed by 1st July 1865 and the coffer dam was removed thereby allowing in the water. The new facilities for the LNWR came into use on the 1st January 1866 at a total cost of £194,538.

In 1870 after complaints by the then Marine Superintendent Capt. Dent of fishing boats taking up precious quay space, the Board of Trade sanctioned the construction of a fish jetty 430ft. (130mtrs.) in length on land near the Pelham Quay. Later when the fish trade decreased the jetty was used as a stand by pier for LNWR steamers.

In the early 1870s additional commerce had started with a LNWR service to Greenore in Ireland, this necessitated a further extension to the inner harbour, this time on the east side. Provisions were made under the Holyhead Harbour Act of 1873 for further dredging of the harbour, construction of berthing facilities and a graving dock some 410ft. in length by 70ft. in width for the repair and maintenance of the LNWR ships. The existing dock opposite Admiralty Pier being to small to accommodate new larger ships. The development also included a goods warehouse, rail facilities for 450 wagons and a public quay with access from the A5 road.

The contract was awarded to Messrs Scott and Edward's of Lytham in November 1874 at a cost of £151,912. Work commenced in 1875 and was completed by 1880 when the new graving dock was opened.

The third and final construction in the inner harbour by the LNWR was the building of a passenger terminal at the southern end of the harbour. This included berthing facilities for four ships, two on the west and east side respectively, a station complex which included covered platforms adjacent to the berthing quays thereby enabling passengers easy access in transferring between train and boat when embarking or disembarking. A five storey red bricked hotel with sixty five bedrooms was also built within the complex offering a facility to passengers who wished to take respite from their journey. Access to the hotel was by both rail and a road leading from the hotel's concourse to a junction with the A5 London Rd.

The building contract was awarded to Messrs J. Parnell and Son at a cost of £64,807, The plans were drawn up in 1876 and work commenced in November 1877 and was completed by 1880. The whole project was officially opened by the Prince of Wales on the 17th June 1880 who had stayed overnight and breakfasted in the hotel. After the official ceremony the Prince embarked on the s.s. *Lily* for a two hour sail along the coast. This was followed by a ceremonial banquet laid out in the new goods warehouse.

To commemorate his visit a large clock was erected in the passenger area situated in the apex of the two berthing quays.

On the operating side further developments that were undertaken were the provision of a Carriage and Wagon depot for the maintenence of rolling stock and a Motive Power depot capable of housing 14 engines.

It is worth noting that the whole inner harbour port was owned by the LNWR, and the CDSP Co. who at that time held the sea mail contract was restricted to the Admiralty Pier for its berthing facilities.

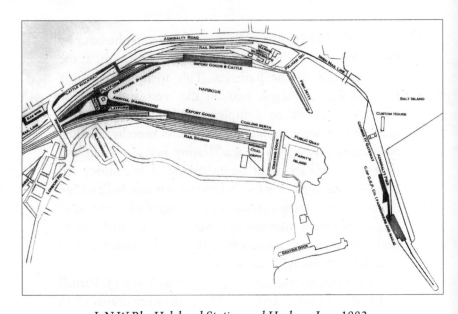

L.N.W.Rly. Holyhead Station and Harbour June 1883
Drawn from the Board of Trade Chart dated Oct. 20th 1888

Author collection
Courtesy Ynys Môn Archives

Station Hotel circa 1900, also showing arrival platform
T. Selby collection

Postcard circa 1907 Holyhead Station
Passengers on Platform 1, embarking on the Day Express Boat
G. S. *Griffiths collection*

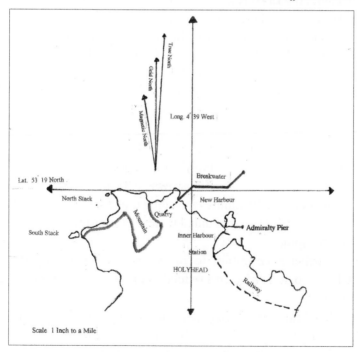

Map of the Holyhead Area circa 1900
Author's collection

Acceleration in Train and Ship Schedules

Minimal improvements were made to the Irish Mail schedules from 1860 until 1883 when the mail contract came up for renewal. Having recently carried out major improvements to the inner harbour, and in anticipation of this the LNWR's tendered for the contract and were successful in their application. This led to an immediate outcry from Irish MP's on behalf of the CDSP Co. at the unfairness of losing the contract after many years of valuable service. Coupled with this was the difficult problem of Irish Home Rule which was being exerted in Ireland at the time. The Government therefore took the conciliatory step to reverse the decision and at the request of the Postmaster General the LNWR was requested to withdraw its tender in favour of the CDSP Co.

The new contract brought with it an acceleration in service. In June 1884 the Down Morning mail left

Euston at	7.15am
Holyhead	1.20pm
Kingstown	5.20pm

Down night mail	Euston	8.25pm
	Holyhead	2.30am
	Kingstown	6.35am

A gain of some 30 minutes travelling time for the night mail, The Up mails were scheduled to arrive in Euston at 5.55am and 6.15pm.

Further acceleration to the service was made by the CDSP Co. in 1885 with a reduction of 20 minutes in the sea crossing.

In addition to improvements to the engines of their ships the CDSP Co. added to their fleet the paddle steamer '*Ireland*' which was capable of 20 knots. On one occasion it made the crossing from Holyhead to Kingstown in 2hrs. 44mins.

Once more in 1895 a further contract fixed for a period of twenty years was agreed by the CDSP Co. and the Post Office. To facilitate the service the CDSO Co. ordered four twin screwed vessels from Laird Bros. of Birkenhead each of 2646tons, 129ft. long (118mtrs.) and with an eight cylinder steam engine generating 9000 horse power producing a speed of 24 knots. Named after the 'Four Provinces' in Ireland, *Ulster, Munster, Leinster,* and *Connaught.* The ships included an on board mail sorting office manned by members of the Dublin Post Office. This led to the replacing off the older four paddle steamers of the same name which were sold off.

The new contract service began on the 1st April 1897

Down night mail		Up night mail	
dep. Euston	8.45pm	dep. Dublin	8.10pm
Holyhead	2.17am	Kingstown	8.40pm
Kingstown	5.55am	Holyhead	12.10am
Dublin	6.25am	Euston	6.10am

Overall time of 9hr 40mins, a reduction of 40 minutes in travelling time. Also to further extend the facilities of the Irish mail 3rd. class passengers were allowed to travel on the mail trains whereas previously only 1st. and 2nd. Passengers were carried. There were no alterations to the day service until 1st August 1898

dep. Euston	8.30am
Holyhead	2.05pm
Kingstown	5.25pm
Dublin	5.55pm

The Up day service was accelerated to the saving of 45mins. (15mins. by sea, and 30mins. by rail).

Meanwhile in this period from 1860 the L.N.W.R.

continued its Day and Night Express Boat service. It replaced its 1848 ships *Anglia, Cambria, Scotia,* and *Hibernia* in 1876 with the *Rose* and *Shamrock,* built by Laird's of Birkenhead, each had a tonnage of 1269 tons and a capability of 20 knots. In 1880 a further two ships were ordered from Laird's the *Lily* and *Violet* with a tonnage of 1035 tons and speed of 19.5 Knots. These four vessels were eventually replaced, when in 1897 the L.N.W.R. upgraded its fleet with four new ships built by Denny's of Dumbarton. The *Cambria* in 1897, *Anglia* 1900, *Hibernia* 1900 and *Scotia* 1902, each had a tonnage of 1872 tons and with a capability of 22knots.

During the years up to 1914 only minimal alterations to the 1897–98 schedules took place and at the outbreak of war sailing's became subject to variable alterations. In the main sea crossings were restricted as far as possible to daylight hours. This precaution was to no avail when at 10am on the 10 October 1918 the *Leinster* on the mail crossing was torpedoed by UB 123 at a position sixteen miles from Kingstown., the torpedo striking the ship in the vicinity of the postal room. The Captain endeavoured to turn the ship 180 degrees to try and make it back to Kingstown when a second torpedo struck the ship which fatally damaged it. The *Leinster* sank with a loss of 501 lives including 21 out of 22 postal sorters.

Another blow to the CDSP Co. was when the *Connaught* which had been requisitioned by the Admiralty as a troop ship was torpedoed and sunk by U48 in the English Channel on 4th March 1917 returning from Le Havre to Southampton after delivering troops. Hit by two torpedoes 3 out of the crew of 77 were killed, the remainder took to the life boats and were saved.

After the war in 1920 the mail contract with the Post Office came up for renewal once more, and again there was intense competition between the CDSP Co. and the LNWR. The tender of the railway company was for £100,000, this time lower by £30,000 than that of its rival and was successful in its application. Subsequently the LNWR was awarded the contract for both land and sea conveyance of the Royal Mail which came into effect on the 28th November 1920. The contract was for sailing's seven days a week with a proviso attached that should the company withdraw it's Sunday sailing's the payment it received would be reduced by £10,400. Also a further clause was added that should the ship fail to sail following the arrival of the Mail train a penalty of £20 per hour would be imposed. The agreed passage time for the sailing's from quay to quay was 2hrs. and 55mins. Unfortunately with the losses incurred during the war of the *Leinster*, and *Connaught* and subsequent loss of the mail contract brought about the demise of the CDSP Co., having held the contract for over seventy years it went out of business. The final sailing by the company in the transportation of 'mails' was on the 27th November 1920 when the *Munster* carried the day mail from Holyhead to Kingstown. The CDSP Co.'s last two ships the *Ulster* and *Munster* were sold off, and finally scrapped four years later in Germany.

The LNWR had also incurred losses during the war, the *Hibernia* renamed *Tara* had been torpedoed and sunk in the Mediterranean, and the *Anglia* converted as a hospital ship was mined and sunk in the English Channel.

At the end of hostilities in 1918 the LNWR ordered four new twin screw turbine ships from Denny's of Dumbarton, again named *Anglia*, *Hibernia Cambria* and *Scotia*, each with a tonnage of 3,400 tons, and 16,000 horse power engines capable of 25 knots. At that time they were the fastest coal burning ships in the country.

The inaugural conveyance of 'mails' by the L.N.W.R. by

sea began on the 28th November 1920, with the 3.50am sailing Holyhead to Kingstown by the *Anglia* which was the only new ship that had come into service in time. The reverse day mail sailing from Kingstown to Holyhead was carried by the *Curraghmore*. In order to fulfill its commitment, the L.N.W.R. had transferred the *Curraghmore* from its Holyhead to Greenore route to supplement the *Anglia* in the mail service until the *Hibernia* came into service a few weeks after the new mail contract had begun. The *Cambria* and *Scotia* came into service in 1921.

So began a contract between the Railway and the Post office that was to last a further eighty years.

The Weedon Rail Crash

On the 14th August 1915 just south of Weedon station which is seven miles north of Blisworth, whilst on the Up line the 8.45am Birmingham to Euston express hauled by

Painting of the C. of D.S.P. Co. R.M.S. Leinster by R. Waring 1900
Torpedoed and sunk by UB 123 on the 10th October 1918
whilst carrying the Day Mail from Dublin to Holyhead
Courtesy Holyhead Martime Museum

C. of D.S.P. Co. R.M.S. Connaught requisitioned by the Admiralty as aTroopship W.W.1.
Torpedoed and sunk by U48 in the English Channel 4th March 1917.

Courtesy of Sea Breezes

L.N.W.R. steamer 'Anglia' requisitioned by the Admiralty as a Hospital ship W.W.1. sunk by mines laid by UC5 in the English Channel 17 November 1915

Mr H. Feltham collection

*Painting by Tudur Roberts of H.M.H.S. Anglia, (L.N.W.R. Anglia)
sinking in the English Channel on the 17th November 1915 after
striking a mine laid by German submarine UC5.
With Destroyer H.M.S. Hazard in the foreground*

Commissioned by the Author

*L.N.W.R. steamer 'Hibernia' re named H.M.S. Tara. Requisitioned
by the Admiralty as an Armed Boarding Steamer W.W.1.
Torpedoed and sunk by U35 in the Gulf of Sollum in the
Mediterranean Sea 5th November 1915*

Mr H. Feltham collection

*Painting by Tudur Roberts of H.M.S. Tara (L.N.W.R. Hibernia)
sinking in the Gulf of Sollum in the Mediterranean Sea on the 5th
November 1915 after being torpedoed by German submarine U35*
Commissioned by the Author

*R.M.S. Scotia built 1920 by Denny's of Dunbarton
Sunk by German aircraft 1st June 1940 during the Dunkirk
evacuation*
Courtesy Capt. W. Lloyd Williams

L.N.W.R. George the Fifth Class locomotive No. 1489 lost a taper pin which fell off the engine. The purpose of the pin was to lock a screwed collar that retained the offside coupling rod to its crank pin. The realisation was that without the taper pin the screwed collar unthreaded itself and the coupling rod came off its crank pin and detached from the engine. In doing so it struck the sleepers on the Down line pushing the track out of alignment. Approaching was the Down 8.30am Euston to Holyhead day Irish Mail, consisting of fifteen coaches and being double headed by two engines, the Renown Class No. 1971 and the Precedent Class No. 1189 which were travelling at 60m.p.h. On reaching the damage track both engines and all the coaches were derailed. The point of derailment was 162yds. (147mtrs.) south of the down signal for Weedon No. 1 signal box between Stowe tunnel and Weedon. Both derailed engines detached from the train and although they remained upright they also separated with engine No. 1971 coming to rest 45yds. (41mtrs.) from the leading engine No. 1189. The remainder of the train derailed with tragic circumstances, the first three coaches were thrown down an embankment on the Down side and were destroyed, the next five coaches went down the embankment on the Up side and were damaged, the next, the dining car although remaining upright had its leading end ripped open including the roof. The last five coaches although derailed remained upright with only slight damage. In all ten passengers were killed and twenty one were injured including the drivers and firemen of both engines, the guard, and five restaurant staff, and thirty three suffered from severe shock.

As a result of the accident inquiry led by Lt. Col. E. Druitt of the Board of Trade it was suggested in future the screwed collars should be given a fail safe devise in order that they could not unscrew if a taper pin was lost.

In his final submission Lt. Col. Druitt stated. 'It will be seen that all the circumstances attending this unfortunate accident were of a most unusual character, viz. The working out of the split pin, the slackening back and falling off of the washer, and the coupling rod dropping and being bent outwards so as to damage the adjoining line, I believe this is only the case on record of an accident having occurred from this last cause.'

In concluding this Chapter it is worth noting an incident on the 12th September 1880 when an attempt was made to wreck the down Irish mail near Bushey, Herts.
*** An explosive charge was placed on the line but fortunately it did not detonate. This prompted the L.N.W.R. to offer a reward of £100 to anyone who could furnish information leading to arrest of those involved, but there was no response. The following year the Fenian scare was at its height, and warnings that both the Irish Mail trains and the Britannia Bridge were threatened, but nothing materialised. (Fenian: Irish Secret Society seeking an independent Irish Republic).
*** Neale Railway Reminiscences Pg. 214

Chapter 11

1921–1964

By 1921 time tables for the Irish mail varied little from those of 1897, with both day and night mails leaving Euston at 8.30am and 8.45pm respectively, arriving at Holyhead at 2.05pm and 2.25am and Dublin at 6pm and 6.30am. The Up day mail also maintained its pre war schedule, whereas the night mail from Dublin departed one hour earlier at 7.10pm. One notable feature however was that mail trains ran non stop between Chester and Holyhead for both up and down day and night mails. Schedule running between the two stations was 1hr. 42mins. for the down mail and 1hr. 44mins. for the up mail.

Night Down Mail			Night Up Mail		
Dep.	Euston	8.45pm	Dep.	Dublin	7.10pm
Dep.	Crewe	12.08am	Dep.	Holyhead	11.11pm
			non stop		
Dep.	Chester	12.43am	Arr.	Chester	12.55am
non stop			Dep.	Chester	1.05am
Arr.	Holyhead	2.25am	Arr.	Crewe	1.35am
Arr.	Dublin	6.35am	Arr.	Euston	5.00am

Until November 1921 the contract for the sea mail service was still with the CDSP Co. berthing at the Mail pier at Holyhead. In November the contract was awarded to the L.N.W.R. which as previously stated sailed from the new inner harbour. It can be noted that after the L.N.W.R. had been given the mail contract for both land and sea, the wooden Mail Pier jetty was no longer required as a berthing facility and with government authority it was eventually dismantled. Another change which took place in the 1920s was that the sorting of mail on board ship ceased on the day mailboat on the 10th March 1923 and on the night mailboat on 21st February 1925.

To also further enhance the Irish Mail train a further facility was the provided for passengers, that of third Class sleeping accommodation which commenced on the 24th September 1928, with each sleeping car having provision for twenty eight passengers.

Also in 1925 saw the withdrawal of the mail steamer Anglia from service due to economic circumstances, and she was laid up in Barrow in Furness, before eventually being broken up. This left only the *Cambria, Hibernia,* and *Scotia* to fulfill the mailboat service.

Holyhead Harbour circa 1923
Courtesy The Royal commission
of the Ancient & Historical Monuments of Wales

Postcard circa 1930 showing L.M.S. Mail Boats Hibernia and Cambria in the departure and arrival berths at Holyhead. In between the clock, which was erected in 1880 on the completion of the new inner harbour, and the Cambria to the right can be seen the barge used for coaling the ships.

C. Chadwick collection

Grouping of the Railways

Prior to the First World War the railways had reached its zenith with just over one hundred and twenty different railway companies, which ranged in scale from the premier the LNWR. to the smallest the Furness Railway.

At the outbreak of war in 1914 the railway network was taken over by the government for the duration, and was not returned to its pre war days until 1921. At this period a government White Paper had been produced which set out a plan of how the British rail system should be operated. Stopping short of full nationalisation a system of 'Grouping' was forecast with the creation of four groups based on geographical area. The financial situation of the railways after the war years was in rather an uncertain state, an eight hour day had been introduced and the wage bill had increased threefold as against those of pre war years.

In 1921 a Railway Bill was passed by Parliament which became the Railways Act of 1921. Subsequently following this a grouping of the rail system came into being on 1st January 1923 with the formation of the Great Western Railway (GWR), London & North Eastern Railway (LNER), London Midland & Scottish Railway (LMS), and the Southern Railway (SR).

It was into the LMS, that the LNWR, was amalgamated along with the following companies, The Midland Railway, Caledonian Railway, Glasgow and South Western Railway, Highland Railway, Furness Railway, North Staffordshire Railway, and the North London Railway. The Lancashire and Yorkshire Railway had already amalgamated with the LNWR. in 1921 therefore automatically became part of the LMS.

In the initial stages the grouping of the LMS, was laid with difficulties, with rivalry, power struggles, and work practices alien to the beliefs of certain railway companies. It was not until October 1927 with the appointment of Sir Joseph Stamp as Chairman of the LMS, that the unification amongst the parties concerned was achieved through his leadership. In 1923 the LMS. was responsible for 6,900 miles track.

Motive Power

By the mid 1920s the LMS had followed the Midland railways small engine policy which were of insufficient power to fulfill the needs of the West Coast Main Line. Mainline trains were often double headed in and out of Euston, whereas the engines of the LNER and GWR out of Kings Cross and Paddington stations respectively were perfectly capable of pulling heavier trains with only one locomotive. At this time the 4-6-0 Class 5P Claughton locomotives were the main stay of the Irish Mail, however they were of 1913 design and although expectations of them pulling upwards of 440 tons without double heading were never realised due to limited performance. Although in the

6ft. 6inch. dw. 4-6-0 Claughton Class 5P No. 1191 'Sir Frank Ree'
Class built 1913-21
In 1922 this class of engine did the trial non stop run
London Euston to Holyhead

Edward Tallbot collection

Unrebuilt 'Royal Scot' No. 6118 'Royal Welch Fusilier'
Awaiting to depart from Holyhead with the 'Up' Day Mail
Built 1927, Rebuilt 1944, Withdrawn 1964

J. Cave MBE collection

1922 the L.M.S. decided to trial a Claughton class loco with a non stop run from London Euston to Holyhead a distance of 263 miles (421km). Leaving Euston at 8.15am it arrived in Holyhead at 2.03pm. On the footplate was a Holyhead

Postcard depicting an 'Up' Irish Mail leaving Conway Tubular Bridge.
Royal Scot Class 4-6-0 No. 46122 'Royal Ulster Rifleman'
Courtesy J. Salmon Ltd.

Re built 'Royal Scot Class' engine.
Departing Holyhead with the 'Up' Day Mail.
Identification uncertain. Displaying 'The Irish Mail' Headboard.
Which was introduced in 1948 when the Railways were
Nationalised.

crew, driver David Noble and fireman William Williams. Nevertheless there were comments from contemporaries at the time as to its capability. This class of engine was replaced between 1930 and 1935.

To overcome the lack of engine power the LMS in 1927 introduced a new class of locomotive, the 4-6-0 Class 6P Royal Scot Class. These engines worked the West Coast Main Line before establishing themselves on the Irish Mail route and were the mainstay of the Irish Mail train for the next thirty years. In all seventy were built, fifty at the North British Locomotive works in Glasgow. No.'s 6100-6149 and a further twenty at the railway's Derby works. No.'s 6150-6169.

These engines had 3 cylinders, each with its set of Walschaert valve gears (piston valves) and parallel boilers each capable of producing 250 psi. superheated. The engines weighed 84tons 18 cwt., and had a wheel diameter of 6ft. 9inches.

In 1943 a complete rebuilding of this class was carried out to further improve performance. Which included taper boilers, double chimneys mounted on a circular smokebox, new frames which were less liable to cracking and new cylinders with better steam passages.

The Royal Scot Class locomotives were named after British Army Regiments and came to be the best all round moderate sized passenger engines in Britain. It was reclassified to 7P in 1951.

The Transition Years

The Irish Mail schedules remained fairly constant during the 1920's and 30's until the outbreak of World War Ii when Holyhead as a port was closed to shipping during the hours of darkness, consequently the night mail was suspended for the duration of the war and also in 1941 the Sunday Day mail service was also suspended.

One unfortunate casualty of the war was the mail steamer *Scotia* which was requisitioned by the Admiralty for the evacuation of Dunkirk. On the 1st June 1940 whilst evacuating 2000 French troops she was bombed and sunk by German aircraft. Although there were casualties, in the main by good fortune most of the crew and troops were rescued by the British destroyer H.M.S. Esk.

In 1947 the *Princess Maud* was transferred to Holyhead from the Stranraer to Larne route to replace the *Scotia* as the relief third mail boat. having had a distinguished war record serving as a troopship out of Southampton, and was seriously damaged during the Dunkirk evacuation. After repairs she returned to troopship duties until the D Day invasion when she carried U.S.Army engineers engaged in clearing beach obstacles.

Built by Denny's of Dumbarton in 1934, the vessel had a gross tonnage of 2886tons, and was a turbine twin screw oil burner, although originally her boilers were coal fired by means of mechanical stokers She was a two class ship certified to carry 1458 passengers and had the distinction of being the first ship in Holyhead that was fitted with radar. In 1947 with a coal crisis throughout the country the *Hibernia* and *Cambria* were for a time taken out of service and the Princess Maud alone maintained the mail contract.

During 1949 the *Hibernia* and *Cambria* were withdrawn from service and eventually broken up. The *Hibernia* left Holyhead on March 30th for Barrow-in-Furness followed by the *Cambria* on May 17th to Milford Haven. They were replaced by a 4th generation *Hibernia* and *Cambria*, diesel driven ships of 5200 gross tonnage built by Harland and Wolff of Belfast, with 10,000hp. engines capable of generating a speed of 21knots. They were a two class ship with a passenger capacity of 2300. The *Hibernia* arrived in Holyhead in April 1949 and made her maiden mail crossing on April 14th with the *Cambria* making her first sailing in May.

Similar to the First World War the railways were taken

'Hibernia' in the departure berth at Holyhead circa 1950's
The station hotel opened in 1880 is seen to the left
Jim Ashby collection

Postcard showing the 'Outward Day Mail' boat leaving Holyhead
circa 1950's
Seen left of picture are, The Custom House, The George IV arch,
and the Admiralty Pier
Author's collection

Holyhead Harbout circa 1960's
D. Lloyd Hughes & D. M. Williams
'The Story of a Port' 1981
Courtesy Mrs Sian Williams

over by the Government and on the 3rd September 1939 a Railway Executive Committee was established to manage the system on behalf of the Ministry of Transport.

At the end of six years of hostilities the railways were in a poor state with both the track and locomotives in much need of repair due to the immense amount of wartime traffic and enemy action. Insufficient time and labour had been available to carry out maintenance on both track and locomotives to the standard which had prevailed before the war.

On the 28th November 1946 a bill was introduced for the Nationalisation of the whole of the transport system for both rail and road facilities. It became law on the 1st January 1948 and the British Transport Commission was set up with the Railway Executive assisting with all rail aspects.

The priority of the time was the provision of new locomotive stock, however with the country deeply in debt due to the war, financial restraints were such that the upgrading of steam to diesel power was not feasible, also the railway workshops had not been upgraded to facilitate such a development on a large scale. Therefore a decision was taken for the production of a 'Standard' class of steam engine, which included a range of '7MT Britannia' 4-6-2 pacific class of engine. In all fifty two were built.

No.'s 70000 to 70024 built in 1951
"   70025 to 70037   "   1952
"   70038 to 70044   "   1953
"   70045 to 70054   "   1954

In 1953 the Britannia class replaced the Royal Scot class on the Irish Mail route, and the following were allocated to the Holyhead shed (No. 6J).

No.'s 70030 "William Wordsworth"
"   70031 "Byron"
"   70032 "Tennyson"
"   70033 "Charles Dickens"
"   70034 "Thomas Hardy"

They each had a BRI tender which had a 4250 gallon

Britannia Class 70004 'William Shakespeare' with the relief day mail negotiating the gradient out of Holyhead, assisted by a banking engine which can be seen in the rear

B. A. Wynne collection

water and a 7ton coal capacity. However the coal capacity of tenders was insufficient for the demands of the Irish Mail by having to re coal on route and in 1954 the engines were replaced by the following which were fitted with the improved BR1D tenders which had a 4725 gallon water and 9ton coal capacity and also curved upper fairings which allowed a smoother airflow over the engine. The tenders were also designed with a steam powered coal pusher which removed the need of the fireman to climb into the tender to pull the coal forward when the engine stationary.

Allocated to Holyhead

No.'s 70045 "Lord Rowallan"
"   70046 un named, eventually named Anzac
"   70047   "
"   70048 "The Territorial Army 1908–1958"
              named in 1958
"   70049 un named, eventually named Solway Firth

Only nine of these BR1D engines were built.

In 1953 a modernisation plan of the whole of the British Railway system was put forward for the replacement of steam by diesel and electrification. This did not happen overnight, the necessary requirements for the development and provision of diesel locomotives and subsequent training of crews was to take until the late 1950s and early 1960s. The final years of steam saw a miscellany of locomotives working the Irish Mail, from Britannia Pacific's through to the Princess Royal Class and Princess Coronation Class of engines.

The last steam hauled Irish Mail out of Euston was on the 4th September 1964, by Britannia Pacific, 70004 *William Shakespeare*.

Dieseliation of the Irish Mail began on 25th April 1960 with the introduction of the English Electric Type C or 4

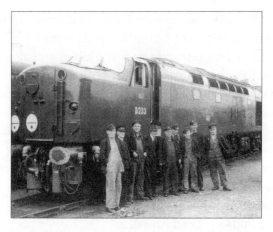

Class 40 diesel at Holyhead, used for driver training 1959.
left to right: Driver C. Bayliss, Inspector F. Taylor,
Driver G. Hayden, Loco Inspector E. Evans,
Driver D. Manley Williams, Driver G. Owen,
Fireman J. G. Williams, Driver I. Hughes, Fireman I. Jones
J. Cave MBE collection

Class D40 diesel engine heading a 'Down' day Irish Mail passing Ty
Croes Anglesey displaying the Irish Mail Headboard
Barry Wynne collection

Class 40 diesels at Holyhead circa 1960's
showing the variants of recognition signs
Courtesy Steve Morris collection

Britannia Pacific No. 70048 'The Territorial Army 1908–1958'
Departing Holyhead with the 'Up' Day Mail
Displaying the 'Irish Mail' headboard, introduced in 1948 after
Nationalisation
Courtesy J. Cave MBE collection

Staff of the Holyhead shed displaying two famous headboards
Courtesy E. N. Kneale

diesel electric locomotive.

In all two hundred of these engines were built between 1958 and 1962 and numbered D200 through to D399. In 1973 they were renumbered 40001 to 40199 to suit the computer operating system and became known as Class 40 engines. All were built at the Vulcan Foundry in Newton-le -Willows except for those bearing the numbers D305 – D324 which were built at the Robert Stephenson and Hawthorn factory in Darlington.

Dimensions

Length 69ft. 18inch. (21.18m)

Width 9ft. (2.74m)

Height 12ft. 10inch. (3.91m)

Weight 133tons (135tonnes)

Top speed 90m.p.h. (140km/h)

In October 1959 D233 was allocated to the Holyhead shed for driver training. and was named *Empress of England* in 1961, after the *Canadian Pacific* steamship liner which sailed out of Liverpool. D233 was renumbered (40033).

During the period of the 1950s and into the 60s the night

mail ran throughout the year, with the British Railways time table for the period 15th June 1959 to 12th June 1960 showing as follow

Winter Schedule

Down Mail		Up Mail	
Dep. Euston	8.45pm	Dep Dun Laoghaire	8.40pm
Dep. Rugby	10.34pm	Arr. Holyhead	11.55pm
Dep. Crewe	12.16am	Dep. Holyhead	1.10am
Dep. Chester	12.54am	Arr. Chester	2.57am
Arr. Holyhead	2.35am	Arr. Crewe	3.24am
		Arr. Rugby	5.03am
Mail Boat Dep.	3.25am	Arr. Euston	6.55am
		Arr. Dun Laoghaire	6.40am

Friday nights only. Dep Euston 8.45pm non stop Arr. Holyhead 2.15am.

Relief Mail Dep. Euston 8.50pm stopping at Rugby, Crewe, Chester, Arr. Holyhead 2.35am.

Mr Rupert Hodginson
Sleeping Car Attendant on the
Irish Mail
Courtesy Mr J. Hodginson

The Day Irish Mail was restricted to the Summer period only from June to September with the Down train departing from Euston at 8.05am and arriving at Holyhead at 1.30pm for the 2.30pm sailing which arrived in Dun Laoghaire at 5.45pm.

The Up day service sailing departed Dun Laoghaire at 8am, arriving at Holyhead 12.35pm with the Up mail train leaving at 1.25pm arriving in Euston at 6.55pm.

During the Summer period the Down night Irish Mail departed Euston at 8.45pm and ran none stop arriving in Holyhead at 2.15am, this was followed by a relief mail which departed Euston at 8.50pm and arrived Holyhead at 2.35am, both for the 3.25am sailing.

The Penmaenmawr Crash

In the early hours of Sunday 27th August 1950 a light goods engine 2-6-0 No. 42885 left Llandudno Junction on the down line tender first for Penmaenmawr to pick up a train of granite ballast from the sidings there, on board were the driver, fireman, and the guard for the train, which was due to leave at 3am. On arrival at Penmaenmawr at 2.52am the engine stopped by the signal box and the guard got off the footplate to speak to the signalman before he crossed into the siding where the ballast train was situated. In response to a hand signal from the signalman the driver moved the light engine along the Down line and over the crossover points on to the Up line where he stopped, he then sounded a whistle to inform the signalman that he was in position to move back into the siding to shackle up with the ballast train. Unfortunately events of confusion and misunderstanding during the next few minutes were to have disastrous consequences. On hearing the whistle the signalman opened the points to the siding and signaled the driver with a white light to enter the sidings where the ballast train was waiting. The time was 2.55am, the signalman on hearing a second whistle (the driver at a later inquiry said there was no second whistle) assumed that the light engine was in the siding and reset the points for the Up Irish mail which was running thirty minutes late having been accepted in his section at 2.50am, he also accepted a Down freight train from Mold Junction. However the light engine was still positioned on the Up line, the driver stating at the inquiry that he never saw the lamp signal from the signalman to move back into the siding. After a wait of two to three minutes the driver saw what was an unmistakable 'back' lamp signal from the guard coming towards the engine from the sidings. On this signal he backed the light engine along the line to enter the sidings as he thought, but stopped when he realised that the engine had passed the points and was still positioned on the Up line. The guard by this time had come up to the engine and the driver inquired 'what was happening'. The guard told him to move forward ahead of the points, stop and sound a whistle to alert the signalman. The driver moved forward accordingly, stopped, and whistled. At the same time the driver noticed that the Down home signal was 'off' and so as not to confuse the driver of the approaching down train told his fireman to get down from the engine to change over the engine lamps to white on the front and red on the tender. At that time there was a shout from the guard that the Irish Mail was coming, the guard then showed a red light back towards the signalbox to warn the signalman that the line was not clear, fortunately the signalman saw the light and promptly put the signals to danger. The driver of the light engine then realised the situation and attempted to move forward to try and clear the oncoming express.

The Irish Mail was being hauled by Royal Scot 46119 Lancashire Fusilier pulling a train of sixteen coaches (14 of steel panel and roof construction and 2 of an all timber structure) and weighing in excess of 495 tons and travelling some 60mph (96km/h). When the driver of the mail train saw the signal turn from green to red he immediately applied the brakes but was unable to stop his engine from crashing into the light engine. On impact the Lancashire

Fusilier stoved itself into the tender of 42885 the light engine detaching its front bogey wheels and the rear wheels of the tender, this derailed the mail engine and although it remained upright the impact thrust forward both engines some 240yds. (218mtrs.) tearing up the track as they went. The brake van immediately behind the engine began pitching violently and detached from the engine then rose in the air and plunged downward onto the damage track, following this the next carriage was the sleeping car made of a wooden construction which smashed into the undercarriage of the break van and was totally wrecked. As for the remainder of the train some carriages remained upright whilst others were thrown on their sides strewn across both the tracks. In all six people were killed, all in the sleeping car and thirty seven others were injured. To further add to the problem the down goods train consisting of a guards van and fifty eight wagons including some carrying ammunition was due to arrive in Penmaenmawr at that time, the signalman therefore immediately put the signals to red on the down line. Driver William Williams of the Irish Mail although injured instructed his fireman John Williams also injured to place detonators on the down line to warn any approaching train. As it happened the driver of the freight train now approaching saw the signals turn from green to red and heard the detonators, braked hard and managed to stop short of the main crash site, although it glanced the side of the Lancashire Fusilier only minor damage was caused.

Driver Williams at the inquiry some eleven days later stated 'I got a clear distant signal, then the next home signal was thrown up in my face and changed from green to red. I slammed on my emergency brakes after seeing the signals change. The train was doing a cut speed of 50mph (80km/h) as the crash came.

Retired Irish Mail driver Mr Vincent Williams then the fireman of the approaching goods train recalls. 'Detonators went off and my driver Mervin Brown shut off steam whilst I applied the brakes, we managed to stop the engine before it reached the main crash site, but it brushed passed the derailed engines which effected little damage. My brother was due to fire the Irish Mail on that day so I jumped down from the footplate and ran to the stationary Lancashire Fusilier to see if the crew were alright, and as it happened my brother had changed his shift with John Williams. I found driver William Williams injured and he said that he had instructed his fireman who was also injured to go and place detonators on the down line to warn any approaching train. I went up the line and found John Williams lying injured by the side of the track.'

The signalman on seeing the crash speedily roused the stationmaster who went to the crash site whilst his wife telephone the emergency services and warned three hospitals in the area to stand by. Many local people came and offered assistance, whilst the local café dispensed free tea and coffee to the survivors, and the station was turned into a casualty area until the ambulances arrived. The uninjured were eventually taken by bus to Llandudno Junction where a special train awaited for them to continue their journey.

Repair gangs from Chester and Crewe arrived on the scene and managed to clear the down line of wreckage by just after midnight Sunday; and both lines were opened by 8.15am on the Monday morning.

The Ministry of Transport's inquiry into the accident headed by Lt. Col. G.R.S. Wilson concluded that the view from the signal box to the junction of the siding was obscured by a foot bridge across the platform and hand signals could not easily be seen therefore this obstruction could lead to misunderstandings and was most certainly the case. The inquiry did however highlight the delay of the light engine crossing from the down to up lines and the attempt to enter the sidings. It was felt that the driver should have made known to the signalman that he was still on the main line and that this delay was finally responsible for the accident. It was also noted*, 'The absence of ground signals at Penmaenmawr was also an important contributory factor and there are many other places, particularly on the former London and North Western Railway system, where shunting movements on running lines depend on their control on hand signals from the box. Where it is found that regular shunting movements are carried out at some distance from the box under hand signals, the provision of fixed signals on the ground should be considered on the merits of each case.'

Note: Accident Report, Clause 48, 27th August 1950

A further conclusion referenced the fact that in a collision it is impossible for any form of carriage construction to avoid severe damage to a heavy train even at a moderately high speed. Further to this it was established that after study of the wreckage that the decision taken by the Railway Executive in introducing Buckeye couplings along with long stop buffers on main line trains was of a sound policy. Unfortunately in this case the coupling between the front brake van and the 1st Class all timber Sleeping Carriage was not of this type and the carriages in the position they were marshalled at 1 and 2 behind the engine and tender experienced the largest shock of impact at the crash. It seemed therefore that a Buckeye coupling might have stopped the whole body of the Sleeping Carriage overriding its underframe which resulted its total destruction and loss of life.

At the resumed Coroner's inquest held at Bangor on the

19th September 1950 a verdict of 'Misadventure' was recorded in the case of the victims. However the jury added the following rider to the verdict. *** 'No single person can be saddled with a guilty act, but that there was serious lack of coordination regarding signalling in the dark which calls upon the railway authorities to make drastic reforms in the signal box system and to introduce a better method of cooperation between the signal box and drivers of engines in cross over or shunting operations'.

As a consequence British Railways built a new signal box opposite the entrance to the siding, which was completed in 1953, also significantly sleeping carriages were marshalled at the rear of the Irish Mail.

*** Ministry of Transport letter 26th September 1950. Brig. C. A. Langley.

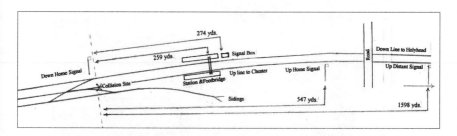

Layout at Penmaenmawr 27th August 1950
Representative Drawing based on V. Anderson & G. Fox's
(Historical Survey of the C&H Rly.) mainline track layout, & the
Accident Report

Author collection

Scene of the 'Irish Mail' crash at Penmaenmawr
20th August 1950

Eryl Crump collection

Engines from the Penmaenmawr crash No.'s 42885 and 46119
'Lancashire Fusilier' at Llandudno Jct. locomotive depot showing
damage to both engines.

H. Rogers Jones collection

Rebuilt Royal Scot No. 46119 'Lancashire Fusilier' repaired after the Penmaenmawr crash. Seen here approaching Llandudno Jct. on a down Class 1 duty

H. Rogers Jones collection

Mr Mervyn Brown   Mr Vincent Williams
Driver & Fireman of the goods train on the Down line of the crash site

Courtesy Mr Vincent Williams Jnr.

Mr R. Williams
Guard of the Irish Mail

Mr William Williams
Driver of the Irish Mail

Courtesy Mr Vincent Williams Jnr.

Mr Vincent Williams former driver of the 'Irish Mail'
at the controls of a diesel engine.
Fireman of the goods train at the Penmaenmawr Crash

Courtesy Mr Vincent Williams Jnr.

The Irish Mail Train Robbery

The Winter of 1963 was one of the worst on record with blizzards sweeping the whole country. On the 20th February the Irish Mail train left Euston at its scheduled time of 8.40pm for the non stop run to Holyhead. The crew on board the train were all from Holyhead. Messrs. Will George Davies (Driver), Llew Roberts, (Fireman), Hywel Owen (Guard), Tom John Thomas (Ticket Collector and Sleeping Car Attendant), Len Tappy (Dining Car Supervisor), Tommy Thomas and Michael Carey (Dining Car Attendants).

The train was marshalled in the following order, Class 40 D type diesel engine, parcel post van, sleeping car, 14 passenger corridor coaches, and rear guards' van which incorporated a wire mesh cage for securing mail bags.

On leaving Euston the guard Mr Hywel Owen locked the door of the guards van, thereby isolating it from the passenger coaches and headed up the train to check everything was in order, and also to assist the ticket collector Mr T. Thomas if required. Because of the terrible weather conditions that night passenger numbers aboard the train were minimal, therefore all checks were reduced and both men returned to the guards' van earlier than normal, As they went through the last carriage next to the van a gang of seven men who were supposedly passengers in that carriage fearlessly attacked them and knock them to the ground constantly beating them, after which they tied them up and threw them into the wire cage in the guards' van, which they had already gained access too, seemingly having had a duplicate key to the van. Following shortly after was the dining car attendant accompanied by a soldier wishing to speak to the guard. As they entered the guard's van both were beaten to the ground by the gang. Not long after one of the dining car attendants arrived in the last carriage to serve teas and he was immediately overwhelmed and thrown into the wire cage. However the second dining car assistant became concerned as to the whereabouts of his colleagues, he therefore locked the dining car and went down the train to see if there was any the problem. When he reached the guard's van which was now locked he knocked on the door and one of the gang shouted at him it's alright it's the police, this was followed by a rather coarse adjective. Immediately he became suspicious and pulled the nearest communication cord to stop the train. The train stopped near Boxmoor in the open countryside.

The normal procedure once a train had stopped was for the guard to climb down on to the track and work his way alongside the train to find out in which the carriage the cord had been pulled, this is indicated by an external disc which is activated when the cord is pulled. The fireman also repeats the same procedure from the front of the train.

Unaware of the happenings on the train, the driver on observing the terrible weather conditions prevailing that night decided to ease the train for inspection into the station at Hemel Hempstead a mile or so away so as to afford protection from the elements. The robbers realising that the train had stopped at the station abandoned any further robbery attempt and fled out of the station taking some packages with them. The captive crew that were not tied up came on to the platform and raised the alarm. The police were soon on the scene and also ambulances to treat the injured. It later became to light that the gang had planned for the train to be halted at signals near Tring by an accomplice, where two getaway cars were situated.

Although extensive inquiries prevailed over the next months no arrests were forthcoming.

Extracts from the *Holyhead and Anglesey Mail* on 22nd February 1963 read as follows:

'Holyhead and Valley railwaymen on the Irish Mail bound for Holyhead on Wednesday night foiled an attempt by seven men to raid the train near Hemel Hempstead Herts.

'The raiders escaped after the alarm was given and the train stopped at Hemel. The police were called and the mail coach was detached from the rest of the train for investigation.

The mail train was a hour and a half late arriving at Holyhead where an ambulance and police were waiting for it.'

What the robbers were after is speculation; some say it was for gems that had been shipped from Amsterdam to Dublin. It was also suggested that a consignment of new £5 notes from the Bank of England to Ireland had been conveyed by the Irish Mail the previous night, so had the gang got their dates wrong.

The Daily Mail of Friday 22nd February 1963 reported: 'For although 27 mail bags were slashed and rifled only 17 registered parcels and envelopes were stolen. One theory is that the highly organised gang were given the "tip off" that one of them contained a fortune.'

However later in the year the Glasgow to London mail train was robbed on the 8th August 1963 of £2-6 million 'The Great Train Robbery'. When the gang responsible for this robbery were caught and questioned they admitted their involvement in the Irish Mail robbery.

Thankfully both Mr Owen and Mr Thomas recovered from their ordeal.

In the book *The Forgotten Train Robbery the Guards' Story* by Arwel Owen, the guard his father Hywel Owen reflects on what might have happened had the Irish Mail remained at a standstill that night in the open countryside. The escaping gang would have had to endure the thick snow and a blizzard in the fields around and possibly would have been caught.

Mr Thomas John Thomas
Ticket Collector and Sleeping
Car Attendant of the Irish Mail
during the robbery
Courtesy Mrs M. Swain Williams

Mr Hywel Owen
Guard of the Irish Mail
during the robbery
Courtesy Mr Hywel Owen

125th ANNIVERSARY
IRISH MAIL
LONDON EUSTON - HOLYHEAD
1ST AUGUST 1848

A JUBILEE CLASS LEAVING EUSTON WITH THE "IRISH MAIL"

Scots Cover Service
B.F.D.C.

Chapter 12

1965-2015

The Britannia Bridge Fire

On the 23rd. May 1970 the Britannia Rail Bridge across the Menai Straits to Anglesey was engulfed in fire and was severely damaged. (See Chapter 4). This effectively cut the rail link between the mainland and Anglesey. Until a new structure was built trains had to terminate at Bangor and a bus service was implemented from there to Llanfair P.G. on Anglesey for passengers to continue their journey to Holyhead by rail.

The severing of the link disrupted the Irish Mail train service through to Holyhead which was temporary withdrawn. The supplement to the 1970 and1971 British Railway timetables stated that the 8.55pm down Irish Mail from Euston and the 1.10am up Irish Mail from Holyhead 'Will Not Run'.

To maintain the mail service to Ireland the mail boats *Hibernia* and *Cambria* were transferred from Holyhead to Heysham in Lancashire, from where they provided a service both for passengers and mails to Dun Laoghaire, a sea journey of some 7½ hours. A mail train although not called the 'Irish Mail' ran daily between Euston and Heysham to connect with the mail boats.

Scheduled as follows:

Down Mail			Up Mail		
Dep.	Euston	9.20pm	Dep. Dun Laoghaire	8.45pm
Arr.	Heysham	2.03am	Arr. Heysham	4.15am
Dep.	Heysham	3.15am	Dep. Heysham	4.50am
Arr.	Dun Laoghaire	10.45am	Arr Euston	9.17am

The resulting fire was so severe that the tubular sections of the bridge sagged and split by the intense heat and had become unsafe for traffic, therefore extensive rebuilding was required.

It was planned that the three stone towers be retained to offer support to the building of new steel arches across the straits in order initially to support the damaged tubes. This first phase of reconstruction was completed by late 1971 and the link was finally opened on 30th January 1972 when the Up line was opened to single line working in both

The Britannia Bridge as originally built in 1850 as seen from the Anglesey side

H. D. Bowtell
Courtesy The Manchester Locomotive Society collection
Archives

The reconstruction of the Britannia Bridge after the fire in 1970
Author's collection

directions and the 'Irish Mail' resumed its regular service.

The *Cambria* having sailed light from Heysham to Dun Laoghaire implemented the 8/45pm sailing from there to Holyhead which connected with the 1.10am up Irish Mail train to Euston. The down mail was re-established leaving Euston at 8/55pm for the 3.25am sailing from Holyhead, which was made by the Holyhead Ferry I acting as relief mail boat for the *Hibernia* which was on lay up.

Reconstruction continued on the Britannia Bridge, with up line open, work began on the down line by removing the tubular sections which were replaced by a steel deck supported by the steel arches on which the track was laid. This was completed by November 1973 and traffic again single line working was transferred over on to the down line on 2nd December 1973. Similarly work began removing the up line tubes, these again were replaced by a steel decking. The work was finally completed by 1974 when both up and down lines were opened to traffic.

To further enhance the bridge, an upper road deck was built above the railway to provide a much needed second road access across the Menai Straits. This began in October

Section of Robert Stephensons' Britannia Tubular Bridge destroyed by fire in 1970. Showing the distinct box girder sections and hand driven rivets.
Author's collection

Present day view of a stone Lion showing the state of pollution from road traffic
Author's collection

1977 and was completed in 1980. This linked the Bangor by pass road to the Llanfair P.G. by pass and eventually became part of the A55 express roadway.

Shipping Services

During the 1960's ownership of the motor car was within the reach of the majority of the population and was becoming an integral part of everyday life. This led to a new concept in travel which was the drive on drive off car ferry. This enabled passengers who had a sea crossing on their journeys to take their cars with them. Whereas previously there was a limitation in the amount of cars that could be carried due to the fact that they were loaded by crane on to conventional ships

July 1965 saw the inauguration of a car ferry service between Holyhead and Dun Laoghaire and this policy move into the car ferry business would as time progressed play a major part in the ultimate withdrawal of the Irish Mail train.

The first purpose built ship to cover this new service was the *Holyhead Ferry I* built by Hawthorne Leslie shipbuilders Ltd. It had a gross tonnage of 3879 tons and a speed of 19½ knots supplied by two sets of oil fired engines. Its carrying capacity was for the loading of 160 cars and 1000 passengers. To facilitate the service a new berth with a stern loading ramp was constructed at the Admiralty Pier and initially due to a delay in the arrival of the new ship the scheduled commencement of the service was carried out by the car ferry *Normania* until the *Holyhead Ferry I* came on station.

In 1976 following a conversion by Swan Hunter shipbuilders the Holyhead Ferry I's car capacity was increased to 205 cars but at a cost of passenger loading which was reduced to 725. After the refit she was renamed Earl Leofric.

Up until 1969 the state owned British Railways managed both land and sea divisions of the railways. However in 1969 B.R. gave a new brand name of 'Sealink' to its Shipping and International Division and up to 1979 the network was known as British Rail / Sealink. From 1979 to1984 Sealink became independent under the name of Sealink UK Ltd., although it was still state owned.

In 1975 the *Cambria* was withdrawn from service and was sold to Greek owners Agapitos Bros. and renamed *Express Apollon.* She was eventually broken up in Mumbai India in 1981. The *Hibernia* was also withdrawn from service in 1976 and was sold to Orri Navigation of Saudi Arabia and renamed *Altaif.* She foundered in the Suez roads also in 1981. In 1975 a new terminal and £650,000 link span was built at the station area of the inner harbour at Holyhead, along with a new customs hall and mail and passenger facilities. This provided the facility for loading

Holyhead and Port circa 1980's

Air Pic
Author's collection

and unloading of cars and commercial vehicles and those of passenger and mail requirements. In 1978 the station hotel was demolished to make way for a new office block and station complex which included a footbridge access to Victoria Rd.

'M. V. Columbia' at the departure berth in Holyhead circa 1981.
Courtesy Capt. I. D. Farrell

To fill the void left by the *Cambria* and *Hibernia* departures, the *Avalon*, *Dover*, and *Duke of Lancaster*, were brought on station until a new passenger and car ferry, the bow and stern loading 8000ton *St. Columba* a two class ship came into service on 27 April 1977.

Built by Aalborg Vaerft of Aaborg Denmark it had the capability of carrying 335 cars or 36 x 40ft. lorries, together with 1,600passengers which could be increased to 2,400 in peak season. By this time the port of Holyhead had an all year round car ferry service to Ireland.

In 1981 a new one class ship the St. David was brought into service and sailed in union with the *St. Columba*. It had a loading capacity of 309 cars or 62 commercial vehicles and 1,000 passengers.

The following ships replaced the *St. Columba* when out of service due to breakdown, overhaul or refit.
Duke of Lancaster 1978
Avalon 1979/80/ renamed *Stena Hengist* 1992
Earl Leofric 1978 ex *Holyhead Ferry I*
Lord Warden 1979
Maid of Kent 1979
Ailsa Princess 1980/81
St. Christopher 1981
Villandry 1983
Lady of Mann
Horsa 1990
Stena Cambria (ex *St.Anselm*) 1991/96

In 1991 the *St. Columba* underwent a major refit and was named *Stena Hibernia*, during her last season of 1996 she was renamed as *Stena Adventurer*.

Subsequent to Sealink working out of Holyhead, in 1981 B&I Ferries an Irish nationalised company introduced a service between Dublin and Holyhead, initially using the car ferry *Connacht* 6,800 gross tonnage, with a carrying capacity of 350cars and 1500passengers, using the berthing terminal on the Admiralty Pier.

Sixty years having passed since the demise of the previous Irish company the City of Dublin Steam Packet Co. service out of Holyhead.

Initially opposition to this new service came from Sealink in the form of a flotilla of small boats on the 2nd March 1981 blockading the harbour at Holyhead, thereby denying the *Connacht* entrance to the harbour, and similar action was taken against the *Leinster* on the 9th March1981 This led to counter measures by the crew of the Dublin based B&I ship *Munster* who in turn prevented the passage of the Sealink Ferry St. David into Dun Laoghaire. With both companies' now at an impasse an agreement was eventually agreed, with shared resources and revenue.

In 1990 the financial position of B&I was causing serious concern, and a decision was taken to privatise the company. This led to it being taken over by the Irish Continental Group Ltd. on the 1st January 1992, a sub division of which is 'Irish Ferries' who now run the Dublin to Holyhead service.

In addition to the introduction of the Car Ferry concept, the 1960,s brought with it a gradual change in freight handling from loose cargo to that of containerisation To facilitate the change the old hydraulic cranes that had been in use in both the East and West warehouses were replaced by four transporter cranes. However by the middle of the1970,s larger freight containers were commonplace and it became necessary to construct a new container terminal, which was concentrated on the East quay of the port to fulfill the requirements needed. In effect this decision to upgrade to a modern freight terminal resulted in the demolition of the warehouses on both sides of the port, along with removal of the transporter cranes. Between the period of the 1970,s and 1980,s saw other changes to the port. Cattle were no longer being shipped on hoof which resulted in the closure of the Cattle Lairages and also there was the closure of the Graving Dock. The dimension of this facility were insufficient for the larger ships that were being brought into service. In effect ships had to go elsewhere for their annual overhaul and repairs. As a consequence the Marine workshops that had served the port for over 100 years were taken out of service, although the buildings still remain. By the 1990,s there was a total withdrawal of all rail freight from Holyhead in favour of Road Haulage by Articulated lorry, and as a result the container terminal was closed in order for further development on the East side of the port to be made. Significantly therefore, the alterations that were made resulted in a large reduction to the rail track system around the port.

Privatisation of Holyhead Harbour

In 1984 Sealink UK Ltd. was sold by the government for the minimal sum of £66 million to Sea Containers of Bermuda. The sale included 37 ships 10 harbours including Holyhead and 10 routes. The new company was known Sealink British Ferries, and a subsidiary company British Ferries Ltd. was set up. In 1989 Stena Line AB of Gothenburg Sweden purchased 8% of Sea Containers shares , and in April 1990 Sealink British Ferries was acquired by Stena Line for £259 million, and the container division of Sealink British Ferries was sold to Tiphook plc. for £321 million. This is a UK headquartered transport services company registered on the London and New York Stock markets, which became the largest marine container leasing business in the 1990's. It brings into perspective the low price of the £66 million the government received for the sale of Sealink UK Ltd.

The new company was known as Sealink Stena Line, in 1993 this was reversed and became known as Stena Sealink Line, by 1995 the company was just named Stena Line.

Rail Services

During the late 1960'sthe 24 hour clock became universal throughout the railway system and all time tables were timed accordingly.

In 1966 the West Coast main line was electrified, and diesel engines hauling the Irish Mail were confined to the

North Wales coast and as far as Crewe. At Crewe diesel engines were changed to electric locomotives for the journey to Euston. A similar procedure was adopted for the reverse journey. Travelling times were greatly reduced, with the down Irish Mail completing the transit time between Euston and Holyhead in 4hrs. 44mins. The up mail took slightly longer in 5hrs. 03mins.

Time Tables for 1973 May to Sept.

Down night mail			Up night mail		
Dep.	Euston	20.55	Dep.	Holyhead	01.10
Arr.	Holyhead	01.39	Arr.	Euston	06.13

Down day mail			Up day mail		
Dep.	Euston	08.45	Dep.	Holyhead	16.05
Arr.	Holyhead	13.18	Arr.	Euston	20.37

During the next decade the Class 40 diesel engines which had worked the Irish Mail after the age of steam were gradually replaced by class 47, 50, 56, diesel engines.

And by the 1980's there were further reductions in transit times.

e.g. Down night mail

Dep. Euston	21.30
Arr. Holyhead	02.28
Dep. Holyhead	03.15
Arr. Dun Laoghaire	06.45

However by the mid 1980's the advent of change had arrived when in 1985 the last train titled 'The Irish Mail' made its final run between Euston and Holyhead on 12th May 1985. Although mail services by rail continued to some extent until 1994, when finally the mail to Ireland conveyed by rail ceased in favour of road transport.

In 1991 Class 43 H.S.T. (High Speed Train) Inter City engines were introduced on the Euston to Holyhead service. Driver training commenced in July 1991 and the H.S.T. service began in September 1991.

This was the start of diesel hauled services throughout between Euston and Holyhead, the first time since electrification of the Crewe to London section of track in 1966.

Privatisation of the Railways

By 1990 the government had sold off nearly all the former state owned industries apart from the national rail network. In January 1993 planning for the privatisation of the British Rail began with the British Rail Transfer Proposals Act1993. Subsequently this led to the creation of Railtrack p.l.c. On the 5th November 1993 the Railway Act 1993 came into being and the operations of the British Railways Board were broken up and sold and privatisation began on 1st. April 1994.

The Railways Bill of 1993 established a complex structure of the railway industry which envisaged a series of rail franchises across the country.

In 1994 the rail contract for the Euston to Holyhead route was taken over by E.W.S.Rail (English, Welsh, and Scottish Rail) until 1997 when Virgin Trains began operating the route, and it is worth noting that both of these companies had no commitment for any mail service to Ireland.

In just over 150years the railways had turned full circle. From private companies at the outset of the railways through to grouping and nationalisation and then back to private ownership.

H.S.S. Stena Explorer berthed at the new terminal in
Holyhead Harbour

Author's collection

Photograph of the 'St. Columbia' during construction at Aaborg
Denmark, which came into service 1977
Holyhead personnel and other dignitaries in the foreground named
as follows:
Mr Rogan B. R. London, Capt. W. Lloyd Williams, David Thorpe,
Michael Wynne, Dewi Reilly, Jack Sharpe, David John Pritchard,
Mr Dickman Naval Architect, Aaborg Yard Representative, John
Emlyn Williams, Roger Rees, Llew bach

Courtesy of Capt. W. Lloyd Williams

New 'Stena' building built on the site of the old Station Hotel
In the centre of the picture can be seen the commemorative clock
erected in 1880, on completion of the Inner Harbour development.
Formerly sited in the apex of the passenger area of the station
between the two berthing quays.

Author's collection

Holyhead Station Hotel built 1880 as part of the Inner Harbout
Development. It closed as a hotel in 1951 and was used as offices
until it was demolished in 1979.

Author's collection

Holyhead Station clock now positioned at the entrance to Holyhead Station. Built to commemorate the Old Harbour Extension opened by the Prince of Wales 1880

Author's collection

The End of an Era

On the 26th October 1996 the *Stena Adventurer* (ex *St. Columba, Stena Hibernia*) was withdrawn from the Holyhead to Dun Laoghaire route in anticipation of a deployment to the Dover to Calais service. However this never materialised, which resulted in the ship being sold to Agapitos Express Ferries of Greece and once more renamed *Express Aphrodite*. The withdrawal of the *Stena Adventurer* thereby closed a chapter in the mail boat association with the port. A new concept in sea travel arrived in the form of the High Speed Ferry HSS 100 named the *Stena Explorer* for the service to Dun Laoghaire. Built at Fennyards in Rauma Finland (Yard No 404). Gross Tonnage 19,638. Powered by four GE Aviation gas turbines with a means of propulsion by 4 Xkamena Type S 'Water Jets'. It came into service in April 1996, with a carrying capacity for 1500 passengers and 375 cars, with a lane space of 800 metres. To accommodate this facility a new passenger and road vehicle terminal was built in the vicinity of the old export warehouse on the East quay of the Holyhead port.

Stena Lines also increased their Holyhead service with the arrival in 2003 of the new *Stena Adventurer* 43,532 gross tonnage, and in 2004 the *Stena Nordica* 24,206 gross tonnage.

In July 1999 Irish Ferries introduced a fast ferry service between Dublin and Holyhead with the arrival of the High

Irish Ferry 'Ulysses' passing the head of the breakwater on entering Holyhead Harbour

Author's collection

Irish Ferry 'Johnathan Swift' berthed alongside the Admiralty Pier In the background can be seen the 'Ulysses' berthed at the new Salt Island terminal

Author's collection

Speed Catamaran *Jonathan Swift,* gross tonnage 5992tons. Incorporating 4 diesel engines, powering 4 Kamewa water jets producing the capability of 40knots. Thereby reducing journey time to 1hr. 49mins. March 2001 saw further expansion by the company when the *Ulysses* gross tonnage 50,938 tons, the largest of all cross channel ferries in the British Isles came into service with the handling capacity for 2000 passengers, 1342 cars and 240 trucks.

Built by Aker Finnyards of Rauma Finland, the same shipyard that built the Stena Explorer.

To accommodate the larger ships a new two tier, two berth terminal was constructed on the northern side of Salt Island, which is shared simultaneously by Irish Ferries and Stena Line.

To access this facility a new bridge was built across the center of the harbour to connect Salt Island with the vehicle

Class 43 H.S.T. No. 43101 named 'Irish Mail' departing Llandudno Junction on the journey from Holyhead to London Euston celebrating the 150th anniversary of the Irish Mail train
Courtesy Mark Lloyd Davies

*Contrasting photographs' showing the redevelopment and reduction
of the rail network at Holyhead*

*D300 (40100) climbs the steep gradient out of Holyhead with an
'Up Day Mail' circa 1960s'*

Courtesy of J. F. A. Hobbs

*Present Day, H.S.T. Virgin Train departing Holyhead 8:55am for
London Euston
The A55 Trunk Road can be seen adjacent to the railway*

Author's collection

Photo showing Holyhead inner harbour at the present day
Author's collection

terminal on the East quay. Also a further pedestrian bridge was built across the harbour which connected the town of Holyhead with the passenger terminal. However these two developments brought with it the isolation of the old rail station berthing areas. In July 2003 the Royal Mail announced the phasing out throughout the whole of the rail network the service of carrying mails by train in favour of road and air distribution. This became effective in March 2004 when rail distribution stopped altogether.

Rail connections to link up with High Speed Ferry continued until 2009 when the connecting passenger rail and sea service between Euston and Dun Laoghaire came to an end. Direct connections between Euston and Holyhead continued but at a reduced level, with the Down trains leaving Euston at 09.10, 17.10, and 18.10, respectively. Whereas the Up trains leave Holyhead at 08.55 and 13.58.

In September 2014 the Stena Explorer was taken out of service and laid up at Holyhead due financial running costs. Eventually it was sold and departed from Holyhead on 1st November 2015 for service in Turkey.

On the 1st August 1998 to commemorate the 150th anniversary of the Irish Mail, a Virgin train H.S.T. 43101 named the 'Irish Mail' worked the 13.38 Holyhead to Euston in celebration of the event. At that time Virgin Trains had a number of named engines, one of which was the 'Irish Mail', eventually all their named trains were phased out by 2002. This in effect brought to an end the era of the Irish Mail, the oldest named train in the world.

Vehicle and passenger ferry Stena Adventurer *departing from Holyhead*
Courtesy of Captain W. Lloyd Williams

'Heritage Run': Royal Scot Class 4-6-0 No. 46100 Royal Scot at Holyhead station 2016
Courtesy of Neil Davies

Bibliography

Robert Stephenson Railway Engineer, John Addyman & Victoria Haworth (North Eastern Railway Assoc.)

Britain's First Trunk Line, Norman W. Webster (Adams & Dart, Bath)

The Chester and Holyhead Railway, Peter E. Baughan (David & Charles, Newton Abbot)

The Chester and Holyhead Railway, J. M. Dunn (The Portland Press for The Oakwood Press)

Royal Mail to Ireland, Edward Watson (E. Arnold 1917 London)

Centenary of the Irish Mail, Haram V. Stewart (Railway Exec. LMR 1948)

The Victorian Railway, Jack Simmons (Thames & Hudson)

Holyhead The Story of a Port, D. Lloyd Hughes & Dorothy Williams

The Land of the Long Long Name, John Lasarus Williams

The Irish Mail, Mike Hitches (Stroud, Sutton 2000)

Holyhead Harbour, George P. Neele (LNWR Gazette)

Holyhead Breakwater and Quarries, E. R. Owens

Trains Boats and Planes, Gareth Rowlands & Alf. Pritchard

Bridges and Ferries, Reg. Chamber Jones(C. Davies Pub. Swansea)

Second Abstract of British Historical, B. R. Mitchell & H. G. Jones Statistics (Cambridge Press 1971)

An Illustrated History of LNWR Engines, Edward Talbot (Oxford Pub. Co.)

The British Locomotive Catalogue, Bertram Baxter (Moorland Pub. Co.) 1825–1923 Vol. 2A & 2B

The Pocket Encyclopedia of British, O. S. Nock (Blanford Press) *Steam Locomotives*

The Crewe Type, D. H. Stuart & B. Reed (Profile Pub. 1971)

North Wales Steam 1927–1964, E. N. Kneale (Oxford Pub. Co.)

An Historical Survey of the Chester and Holyhead Railway, V. R. Anderson & G. K. Fox (Oxford Pub Co.)

Recollections of a Steam Era, D. Rogers Jones. Colwyn Bay.

North Wales Coast Diesels, Steve Morris (Ty Mawr Pub.)

Claughton and Patriot 4-6-0s, G. Toms & R. J. Essary) E8E/452 N.R.M.

Car Ferry to HSS, Miles Cowsill & John H. Hendy (Ferry Pub. Narbeth)

Car Ferries of the Irish Sea 1954–2004, Colourpoint Bks. Newtownards

Sea Breezes, July 1961,

The Forgotten Train Robbery, "The Guards Story" Arwell Owen (Amazon/Kindle)

An Ambitious Voyage, Miles Cowsill & Justin Merrigan (Ferry Pub. I.O.M.)

Pears Cyclopedia

Locomotive Philatelica

Other sources

Archivists National Railway Museum. York.

Archivists Ynys Mon Archives & Record Office. Llangefni.

Archivists Gwynedd Archives & Record Office. Caernarvon.

London & North Western Railway Society

L&NW Railway Gazette

LMS Magazine

Holyhead and Anglesey Mail

North Wales Chronicle

Bridge Books

J. Salmon Ltd.

Acknowledgements

Holyhead Maritime Museum
Staff of the Holyhead Library
L.N.W.R. Society
North Wales Chronicle
National Library of Wales Aberystwyth
Daily Post
Sea Breezes
Ferry Publications
Ty Mawr Publishers
C. Davies Publishers
David & Charles Publishers
North Eastern Railway Assoc.
National Trust, Penrhyn Castle, Bangor
Virgin Trains
D. B. Schenker Rail (UK) Ltd.
Manchester Locomotive Society
County Stationers Holyhead

Personal Acknowledgements

Messrs: Edward Talbot & Norman Lee, (L.N.W.R.Soc.)
Mr John Cave. M.B.E, Mr Vincent Williams (Irish Mail Driver),
Mr Trevor Selby, Capt. W Lloyd Williams, Capt I. D. Farrell. Mr
Ian Fenwick (Irish Ferries).
Messrs: D. Rogers Jones, Hywel Owen, Arwel Owen, E. N.
Kneale, Steve Morris, Barry Wynne, J. Clay, Jim Ashby, P. E.
Baughan, J. M. Dunn, John Hobbs, Mark Lloyd Davies, Andrew
Martin, Eryl Crump, Geriant S. Griffith.
J. Addyman and Ms V. Howorth.
E. Anthony, G. Van Weert, H. M.Williams.
Mrs Sian Murphy, Mrs Mavis Swain-Williams, Mrs Rose
Arkwright.
Also my gratitude to Mr Trevor Selby for his invaluable
photographic assistance.

In producing this book I would like to thank all the persons, institutions and books in which I have consulted, and for permission to reproduce pictures and illustrations. If inadvertently an error of any nature has occurred or acknowledgement omitted I sincerely wish to apologise.

References

Chapter 1
Holyhead The Story of a Port pg. 20, 21, 43, 59-73
The Chester and Holyhead Rly. (Baughan) pg. 11-22
The Chester and Holyhead Rly. (Dunn) pg. 5-8
Royal Mail to Ireland. Pg. 21, 22, 24, 30, 43, 49, 122, 142-147
Centenary of the Irish Mail pg. 8, 9, 12
Land of the Long Long Name pg. 7-16
L&NW Railway Gazette pg. 113, 114
Trains Boats and Planes pg. 17, 29, 31
Bridges and Ferries pg. 19, 21-24
Thomas Telford Wikipedia
Menai Suspension Bridge Wikipedia
Copper in Wales   "
Roman Britain   "
Penmaenmawr   "
British Archaeology Magazine 2002

Chapter 2
Pears Cyclopedia 1972–73 pg. B57, B60, B63
Locomotive Philatelica
Pocket Encyclopedia of British Steam Loco's
Penydarren   Wikipedia
Stockton and Darlington Rly.   "
George Stephenson   "
James Watt   "
Edward Pease   "
The Rocket   "

Chapter 3
Robert Stephenson Railway Engineer pg. 55-79, 101
Robert Stephenson, Planning and Construction of the L.&B. Rly.
London and Birmingham Rly. Wikipedia
Britains First Trunk Line pg. 23, 39-48, 61-63, 90-95, 118, 126
Grand Junction Rly.   Wikipedia

Crewe Railway Station   Wikipedia
Chester and Crewe Rly.   "
Chester and Crewe Rly. pg. 19, 20
The Chester and Holyhead Rly. (Baughan) pg. 23-30, 44-46, 69-73, 228-231
The Chester and Holyhead Rly. (Dunn) pg. 29, 44, 45
The Chester and Holyhead Rly.   Wikipedia
The North Wales Coast History   "

Chapter 4
Robert Stephenson Railway engineer pg.106, 101-120, 153-157
The Chester and Holyhead Rly. (Baughan) pg. 104-142
The Chester and Holyhead Railway (Dunn) pg. 9, 10, 17, 18, 23-26
Historical Survey of the C.& H. Rly. (Anderson & Fox)
The Iron Tubular Bridge over the River Conway Wikipedia
Britannia Bridge Wikipedia
North Wales Chronicle 1850
Anglesey County Archives

Chapter 5
The Victorian Rly. Pg. 219-221
The Centenary of the Irish Mail pg. 12

Chapter 6
Britains First Trunk Line pg. 169
The Victorian Rly. pg. 346
London & North Western Rly. Wikipedia
Trent Valley Line   "

Chapter 7
The Chester and Holyhead Rly. pg. 143-157
The Centenary of the Irish mail pg. 14-21
Sea Breezes July 1961 (Article by A. C. Yeats) pg. 29 to34
An Ambitious Voyage pg. 33-34

Chapter 8
The Chester and Holyhead Rly. (Baughan) pg. 148, 193
The Chester and Holyhead Rly. (Dunn) pg. 28, 29
The Centenary of the Irish mail pg. 20-23
L.M.S. Magazine pg. 279
National Railway Museum
Anglesey County Archives
North Wales Chronicle (1848)

Chapter 9
An Illustrated History of L.N.W.R. engines (Talbot)
The Chester and Holyhead Rly. (Baughan) pg. 190-191
The Chester and Holyhead Rly. (Dunn) pg. 37, 38, 39
The British Locomotive Catalogue 1825–1923. Vol. "2A & "B
Locomotives of the L.N.W.R. Wikipedia
A. McConnell "Bloomer". Wikipedia
Locomotive Philatelica

Chapter 10
The Chester and Holyhead Rly. (Baughan) pg. 178, 179, 203, 221-224, 237-242, 284
The Chester and Holyhead Rly. (Dunn) pg. 13, 14, 24, 28, 29, 30, 45
The Centenary of the Irish mail pg. 19-27
The Story of a Port pg. 89-94
The Holyhead Breakwater and Quarries pg. 11-27
Trains Boats and Planes pg. 51-58
L.&N.W. Gazette pg. 141
National Railway Museum
Board of Trade Report Abergele Disaster
North Wales Chronicle (1868)
Board of Trade Report Accident at Tamworth
Extract for the Accident at Tamworth
Sea Breezes January 1967 pg. 44
Board of Trade Report Weedon Accident
Weedon Rail Crash Wikipedia
Anglesey County Archives

Chapter 11
Centenary of the Irish Mail pg. 29-31
The L.& N.W.R. Claughtons pg. 17-18
National Railway Museum
Min. of Transport Report Penmaenmawr Accident
North Wales Coast Diesels
L.M.S. Royal Scot Class   Wikipedia
Britannia Class 7MT   "
British Rail Class 40   "
The Irish Mail (Hitches)
Historical Survey of the C& H Rly. (Anderson & Fox)
Sea Breezes January 1967 (Article by A. Cyril Yeates) pg. 47-49.
The Forgotten Train Robbery the Guard's Story
Holyhead and Anglesey Mail
The Daily Mail (Article)
Locomotive Philatelica
Pocket Encyclopedia of Steam Locomotives
The Daily Express (Article)

Chapter 12
Bridges and Ferries pg. 62-63
Historical Survey of the C&H Rly. (Anderson & Fox)
Gwynedd County Archives
Car Ferry to HSS (Cowsill & Hendy)
Car Ferries of the Irish Sea 1954–2004
Privatisation of British Rail Wikipedia
An Ambitious Voyage pg. 60-64